Practical Creativity at Key Stages 1 and 2

Primary school teachers looking for practical ways to incorporate drama, dance, art and literacy into their curriculum will be inspired and enthused by the range of ideas presented in this highly practical activity-based book.

The book is helpfully divided into ten themed areas, touching on almost all aspects of the curriculum, for example Materials, History, Feelings and Stories. Each theme's educational value is explored, and is fully supported by:

*   Suggested suitable age/ability ranges and numbers of children
*   Materials and equipment needed
*   How to run the activity
*   Tips, advice and troubleshooting

Including photocopiable sheets for direct use in the classroom, this book effortlessly dispels the mystery surrounding the teaching of creative and expressive arts for the non-specialist and offers additional ideas for teachers already confident in these areas. It will be a valuable resource which can be referred to time and time again for fresh inspiration and ideas.

Jane Bower is a practising primary teacher and independent arts advisor, who works with children and delivers staff Inset courses and training courses across the UK.

Practical Creativity at Key Stages 1 and 2

Forty inspiring lessons in drama, dance, art and literacy

Jane Bower

with illustrations by Leonard Bower

Routledge
Taylor & Francis Group

LONDON AND NEW YORK

First published 2005
by Routledge
2 Park Square, Milton Park, Abingdon, Oxon OX14 4RN

Simultaneously published in the USA and Canada
by Routledge
270 Madison Ave, New York NY 10016

Routledge is an imprint of the Taylor & Francis Group

© 2005 Jane Bower

Typeset in Baskerville by
Keystroke, Jacaranda Lodge, Wolverhampton
Printed and bound in Great Britain by
Bell and Bain Ltd, Glasgow

British Library Cataloguing in Publication Data
A catalogue record for this book is available from the British Library

Library of Congress Cataloging in Publication Data
A catalog record for this book has been requested

ISBN 0–415–34285–6

For Len and Sadie Bower, the two remarkable
art teachers who are my parents

Contents

Preface

About this book

This book is a collection of forty practical, creative lesson plans in drama, dance, art and literacy designed for the primary teacher. The intention has been to provide clear, exciting, manageable ideas for specialists and non-specialists in the arts. All the lessons have been tried and tested, some many times, in different schools and with different age ranges and abilities.

Although lessons are described in full and can be taught as specified, it is my hope that teachers will see ways of adapting my ideas to other topics, and will make links with other curriculum areas. The chapter headings have been chosen with this in mind, and each chapter begins with a short introduction to the theme.

Each chapter is divided into four sections on drama, dance, art and literacy. Each section contains a detailed lesson plan listing what you need, the suggested age range, whether the activity is for a whole class or group, and how to introduce and teach the activity. Each lesson is followed by further ideas or extension activities. The lessons and further ideas are listed on the Contents page together with suggested age ranges for each. The age ranges suggested are for guidance only, as classes and abilities vary greatly. Many of the activities can be adapted for other age ranges and may serve as useful starting points for teachers' own ideas.

At the beginning of the book are notes on drama, dance, art and literacy to give general guidelines about approaching each area. At the back of the book can be found a list of further books and workpacks for teachers on related subjects.

About the author

Jane Bower has taught in primary schools since 1979. The first nine years of her career were as a Years 3–4 class teacher in Lancashire, during which time she wrote stories for BBC's *Play School*. She then became Co-ordinator of Expressive Arts for four primary schools in the Lake District before taking up the post of Expressive Arts Advisory Teacher for South Cambridgeshire primary schools. Redundancy in 1993 led to her establishing herself as an independent Arts advisory teacher to primary schools, and she now works countrywide, has held a part-time post as a teacher of art to Reception, Years 1 and 2 for six years and teaches art to trainee teachers at Homerton College, Cambridge.

Jane writes regularly on practical arts activities for *Child Education, Junior Education* and *Junior Focus, Infant Projects*, and has also written for *Early Years Educator* and *Five to Seven*. She is the author of other books and workpacks, including teachers' packs for NES Arnold and to accompany BBC Radio Drama for schools. She also works professionally as an actress, writing and performing one-woman shows on the lives of remarkable women, and as an artist in residence, producing mural and ceramic commissions for primary schools, but first and foremost regards herself as a primary teacher. Jane is available to work in your school with children or for staff Inset. She can be contacted at jbower@fish.co.uk

Acknowledgements

The drama activity 'A magic carpet ride', first appeared in a different format as an article in the September 2000 issue of *Child Education*.

The Aboriginal journey prints project, with examples of children's work, first appeared in a different format in the February 2001 edition of *Child Education*.

The drama activity 'The Land of Banned Birthdays' first appeared in Jane Bower's book *Ways into Drama* (see Suggested Further Reading) and is used here with the publisher's permission.

The art activity, 'Lonely shapes', and further art activities based on poem/painting combinations first appeared in a different format in *Child Education*, October 2002–January 2003.

The poem *When I'm Lonely* is by the author.

The poem *The Calendar* by Barbara Euphan Todd is used by permission of A.M. Heath and Co. Ltd.

Introduction

Notes on Drama

For me, drama should not be seen as a slot in the timetable, but as a learning medium which can be used to approach a wide range of subjects and curriculum areas. It has been demonstrated that humans retain knowledge for the longest time when they learn by personal involvement and practice by doing, rather than reading, watching or listening to a speaker. Drama enables children to engage in practical experiences which may feel intensely real. As such it is an extremely valuable learning medium, but since it deals with emotions must be handled with sensitivity. For this reason it is important to finish each session with a discussion or winding down activity to help the class return to reality and consolidate their shared experience. Suggestions for these are given in the drama sections of the book.

Similarly, it is essential during the session to make clear when drama is taking place and when it is not. This is not only true for young children, who may be confused or even frightened if they are unsure what is real and what is imagined, but also applies to older children, especially if the drama is exploring a serious subject such as a Victorian classroom or being an evacuee. The method I use, and to which I refer in the book, is very simple. At the beginning of the session I sit on a chair. Whenever I sit on this chair, I am myself, the teacher, and the children are themselves and sit in front of me. Whenever I rise from the chair during the session, the drama begins, and we become other characters in another situation. We probably look and sound no different, but inside we have changed. When I sit down on the chair again at any time, this is a signal that the drama has stopped and that children should return and sit down. This dispenses with the need for shouting or clapping, and can be used to stop the drama for any reason – discussion, discipline problem, end of lesson or urgent message!

For further material on approaching drama and its value as a teaching method, see my book *Ways Into Drama* (Suggested Further Reading).

Notes on Dance

My aim when teaching children through dance is to help them to see it as a language; a way of using the body to tell a story or convey feelings to others. The dances in this book are recorded in choreographed form for clarity, but it should be emphasised that they were all gradually built up by myself and the various children with whom I worked, and evolved from particular starting points we explored together.

Sadly it has not proved possible to include recordings with this publication, but in each case the original pieces used are listed as the 'choreographed music'. In case these prove difficult to obtain, other suitable pieces are listed as 'suggested alternative music'. Clearly the choreography will not fit precisely with the alternative pieces, but my hope is that teachers will feel able and inspired to adapt their own and their pupils' ideas as well as to use my choreography. In some cases the same piece of music is suggested for a different occasion, to enable you to get the most out of it if you have gone to the trouble of buying it!

Notes on Art

The art activities in this book have been chosen with the aim of offering children an opportunity to use a variety of techniques and media, both two and three dimensional, including printing, dyeing, painting, collage and modelling with different materials. The activities link with other curriculum areas such as design technology, science and history, as well as with the drama, dance and literacy activities. There are also references to the work of other artists, cultures and times.

Notes on Literacy

The activities given are intended to complement or form part of the literacy hour. In the main they are focused on reading and writing, but inevitably incorporate speaking and listening skills, and are designed to give children experience of writing in different styles such as letters, diaries and newspapers. The ideas are readily adaptable to other topics and curriculum areas.

Chapter 1

Paintings

Paintings are a source of pleasure, but can offer much more to children's learning. They can provide historical evidence or provoke new ways of thinking about a subject. They can evoke other times, bring about a range of emotions or inspire a desire to paint. This chapter gives four approaches to exploring paintings by four very different artists. The ideas are designed to be adaptable for use with other artists and paintings.

Drama

Wright of Derby – Entering a painting

Entering a painting through drama allows children to enter another world and become involved in its problems, pleasures and decisions.

Suitable for   Whole class, Reception–Year 6 – the drama can be led at different appropriate levels.

You will need   A reproduction of *The Blacksmith's Shop* painted by Wright of Derby in 1771; other reproductions (optional, see *Further ideas*, below).

Introduction

You may wish to give children some background about the artist. Joseph Wright (1734–1797) was associated with his home town of Derby throughout his life. He began as a portrait artist but in 1765 became fascinated by the effect of light, and moved to scientific subjects. Nothing like his work had ever been seen before and he became famous for his 'candle-lights', as his paintings were known. Later in life he visited Italy and continued to explore light, painting moonlit scenes and Vesuvius erupting.

   Study the painting very closely, observing as many details as possible. Discuss exactly what each person might be doing and note what tools and equipment are being used. Why is the metal so white and what is the source of heat? What kind of building are the smiths working in and why might this be? What evidence is there of their previous or ongoing work?

   Having established facts about the shop, now turn to their effects. What problems might there be in this scene? The faces of the people show varied emotions, but none look happy. The state of the building is very poor. Why are they having to work at night?

The drama

Stand up to signal that the drama has started (see Notes on Drama p. 1) and lead the children into the picture, perhaps by opening the imaginary door of the shop. It is wiser to remain as observers rather than trying to talk to the characters in the painting – this often leads to children putting on voices and making the characters say less than helpful things! Instead, you can say that we must not interrupt as they are obviously busy, but maybe we could help. What needs doing?

You can use your own ideas here but also any valuable ideas which come from the children. (It may help if they work in small groups so that they can engage in a task together.) There seem to be two areas where people are heating metal – go and see if there are others. Go out into the cold and cut wood with an axe. Bring it in and stoke up the fires. A boy seems to have been hurt – can anyone treat burns? Drag in more heavy bars of metal and learn to hold them in the fire using protective leather gloves and pincers. The people in the picture look tired and stressed – can anyone prepare a meal for them?

After a short time of activity, you can call the class together and ask what each group has been doing. Children may offer extra information here, or this could come from you. For example, you might say that while they have all been working you spoke to the elderly person sitting in the corner who told you that the local squire is having a grand party attended by royalty, and not only does he want all his horses to be reshod but he has also commissioned six enormous wrought iron gates with his family crest across them. Time is running out – the family has been working every night this week. Trade recently has not been good and they desperately need this commission. If the squire is pleased, the money will be enough to mend the roof and buy better equipment. If he is not pleased he will not pay a penny and the business will have to close.

Back to work – some go to the squire's estate to check the measurements of the gates – what a disaster if they don't fit! Some go to the squire's stables to fetch his horses and hold them while others fit and nail on the shoes. Water is constantly needed from the pump for safety and to cool the metal when it is in shape. Others work on the finished design for the gates (you can have actual pencils and paper for this) and take them to the blacksmiths.

At a suitable point, sit down to come out of the drama and allow the children to return to you. Finish the session by discussing what the result of your labours might have been. If time permits, and the squire is pleased, you might be invited to his grand party to view his fine horses and gates for yourselves. Finally, end the lesson quietly by having one more look at the painting and discussing whether the drama has changed the way in which you view it.

Further ideas (Key Stage 1)

Gallery For younger children with a shorter attention span you may prefer to hang more than one picture around the working space and pretend you are visiting a gallery. After looking closely at the first painting, discussing it and entering it you can move to another one and do the same, experiencing each for a shorter time. Paintings particularly suited to this approach are Canaletto's *The Stonemason's Yard*, late 1720s, (which can be approached in a very similar way to the above session); Bruegel's *Children's Games*, 1560 (ideal for Reception–Year 2); Toulouse Lautrec's *At the Circus Fernando* (1888) and the Limbourg brothers' calendar *Les Très Riches Heures du Duc de Berry*, circa 1413 (choose the months which show medieval farming methods in the greatest detail). However, as in all such lessons, quality is better than quantity and it is valuable to explore one painting to the full before moving to another.

The Blacksmith's Shop and *The Stonemason's Yard* also make excellent drama subjects for projects on Materials, the subject of another chapter of this book, offering contrasts in the ways in which metal and stone behave.

Dance

L. S. Lowry – A 'layered' dance

This dance aims to help children's understanding of the paintings of L. S. Lowry, exploring their layers from background to foreground and evoking their sombre mood.

Suitable for   Whole class, Years 2–6.

You will need   Reproductions of Lowry's cityscape paintings such as *Our Town* (1941), *The Pond* (1950) or *Industrial Landscape* (1955). Choreographed music: Philip Glass, *In the Upper Room*, Dance I. Suggested alternative music: Other works by Philip Glass, such as the *Low Symphony, Concerto for Violin and Orchestra* (2nd movement), Henryk Gorecki, *Symphony No. 3* (2nd movement), or Bach's *Air on a G String*. The mood should be repetitive, sombre, slightly monotonous and depressing to echo the paintings.

Introduction

Study the paintings with the children. The amount of background information you choose to explain will vary according to their age and ability. Lowry was a lonely man who tolerated his job as a rent collector only to please his parents, but his real love was for drawing and painting. His work portrays Salford during the Depression, the second world war and its aftermath, and is characterised by a muted colour range and atmosphere of gloom. A city is endlessly changing and yet repeating itself; buildings are erected, demolished and new ones erected, people come and go, visiting the same places and performing the same tasks each day. The music should help to evoke this.

Look at how the paintings are built up in layers, with the gaunt skylines of buildings in the background, the grim mill chimneys rising up, and the small huddles of people moving like ants in the foreground. Explain that in the dance we are going to become the layers of the painting – our bodies will become the paint being put on the canvas.

The dance

Divide the class into four groups. It may be helpful visually to group the children by height, with the tallest in Group 1 and the shortest in Group 4. Group 1 kneels in a straight line along the back of the dance space, facing the front. Group 2 kneels in a line in front of them, then Group 3 and Group 4. At the start of the dance all children bend their heads down over their knees.

0.00   When the music begins the back children (Group 1) slowly rise, taking each others' hands as they do so. Their joined hands can be positioned to depict a variety of roofs – square, domed, zigzag – as in Lowry's paintings (see Figure 1). Allow 17 seconds of music for this.

0.17   When Group 1 is standing and forming their skyline they remain still while Group 2 slowly rises. The pattern is repeated until all four groups are standing. (Group 3 rises at **0.33** – see Figure 1 overleaf – Group 4 at **0.51**.) Encourage expressionless faces, looking straight ahead. Arm positions can be worked out beforehand so that interesting layers of contrasting shapes are built up.

1.07   Silence. The full skyline is held still. During the first eight beats of the next section of the music, all children should release hands, float them down to their sides (don't just let them drop as this destroys the atmosphere somewhat!) and crouch down on toes and hands. Immediately grow into tall, straight mill chimneys.

1.14   The chimneys should have grown in time for these singing, floaty chords. On these chords it is most effective if all children float their arms horizontally across their bodies, all in the same direction, say to the left of the room, to resemble the smoke from the chimneys. As the music wavers between two repeated notes the fingers and wrists can be gently wafted to bring movement to the smoke.

Figure 1 The Lowry dance at **0.33**

The rest of the dance can use as much or as little of the music as you wish, as the piece is long enough to allow for development, or can be faded down to end the dance. Children split into groups of four to six. The groups should move smoothly into separate areas of the space to give a balanced composition. Each group chooses their own way to depict a building rising and falling. This needs to be worked on so that all the buildings are different (pointed, square, round, tall, squat, etc.) and all are erected and demolished at different rates, so that there is constant interest and variety for the onlooker. Encourage a smoothness to the action, with buildings 'melting' up and down as if they were being painted, rather than jerking. The aim is to depict the endless growing and evolving of the city landscape.

After a suitable length of time the buildings melt apart and the children become individual people. Ideally they should base themselves on an actual person in a Lowry painting. They may move separately or in groups, pushing prams, walking dogs, etc., but the overall effect should be worked on so that (a) all children are moving at the same speed (b) they are using all the available space, and not just walking round in circles, and (c) that they are imitating the particular stance so typical of Lowry's figures – slightly leaning forward, with expressionless faces. There is a strange mix of aimlessness and purposefulness about Lowry's figures which should be aimed for as far as possible.

The figures form the final layer of the painting, so after this the whole painting can be composed. (Again, encourage 'melting' smoothly into the next position – this melting should be seen as part of the dance and not simply a gap between sections.) Some children take their places at the back and form a skyline; in front of them stands a line of children as chimneys with floating smoke; in front of them two or three buildings grow, and in the foreground a few children continue to depict the walking figures. Fade the music down gradually and as it disappears all children should freeze, and the finished painting is seen.

Further ideas

Layers Many paintings are composed of layers from background to foreground. Try the layered dance approach to portray Monet's garden, the paintings of Pieter Breugel, or Dali's *The Metamorphosis of Narcissus*.

Art

Pablo Picasso – Portraits

Children are encouraged to view and create new versions of the human face through the work of Pablo Picasso.

Suitable for   Whole class or group, Reception–Year 6.

You will need   Reproductions of Picasso's paintings *Les Demoiselles d'Avignon* (1907) and *The Dream* (1932). Other very useful additions are *Weeping Woman* (1937), *Nude in a Red Armchair* (1932) and *Guernica* (1937). (You may wish to mask off all but the faces in the paintings at first, in order to focus the attention solely on them.) Large and small brushes; neutral sugar paper; pale chalk; printing trays or plates; paints.

Introduction

Look at the faces in the Picasso paintings. Do they have anything in common? Children may comment that they are not realistic, and notice that areas of them are outlined in black. Often the face is nearly bisected, as in *The Dream*, so that the full face and the profile can be seen at the same time. (This is a good opportunity to introduce the words 'profile' and 'bisect' to children who are unfamiliar with them, as they can use them when planning their painting.) Why might Picasso have painted faces in this way? Suggestions might be that there are two sides to our personality, that Picasso is trying to show every part of the face at once to show the whole person, and that he is using the parts of the face to form a design or a pattern rather than a straight-forward representation. He himself said: 'I give man an image of himself whose elements are collected from among the usual way of seeing things in traditional painting and then reassembled in a fashion that is unexpected and disturbing enough to make it impossible for him to escape the questions it raises'. By rearranging the parts of the face he often reveals the true feelings of the person, as in *Weeping Woman* and *Guernica*.

The art activity

First, help the children to decide on the feeling they want to show in the face they will create. Is it showing anger, fear, joy, loneliness? Or is it going to show two contrasting sides? Which colours would help to put these feelings over?

The children then use chalk to sketch a large, simple facial outline on the paper. (Chalk is better than pencil as it does not show through the paint and any errors can be blurred with the hand rather than rubbed with a rubber, which creates a rough texture on the paper.) Encourage variations on the traditional – perhaps a profile at both sides, a bisected profile or features such as eyes and ears placed asymmetrically or used as a design (three eyes down one side of the face, for example.)

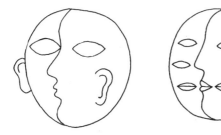

Figure 2 Ideas for initial sketches

Having discussed and chosen appropriate colours, fill in the areas of the face with the large brush, making sure the paint is thick, starting with the palest colours and working towards the darker ones (this avoids constant washing of the brush and therefore constant changing of water.) When dry enough, use the smaller brush for outlining selected areas in black. Further detail or patterning can then be added as desired.

When the face is finished, turn the children's attention to the background. Notice how in *The Dream* the background is also bisected into two very contrasting halves – green with a simple pattern and red with a complex pattern. Notice also how Picasso balances the colours in the picture. If there is some yellow on one side, there is some yellow at the other. The purple line on the woman's neck balances the purple around her waist. Even her necklace changes colour half way along to maintain this balance. Picasso is careful to choose colours which will make the woman stand out against them.

The children can use the chalk to mark in their background patterns, and choose colours which balance each other and which make their face show up clearly.

Further ideas (Reception–Year 6)

Face masks Some of the faces in *Les Demoiselles d'Avignon* were inspired by African masks. Use examples or photographs of such masks to stimulate the making of faces from simple rolled-out ovals of clay. Eyes and mouths can be cut out or built on and further marks or decoration added before firing.

Literacy

Gwen John – Imagining a letter

Studying the clues in a painting to understand its meaning – in this case, deciding on the content of the letter held by the sitter.

Suitable for Whole class or group; Years 4–6 for the writing activity; the discussion is also suitable for younger children.

You will need A reproduction of *The Convalescent* by Gwen John (1920); writing materials.

Introduction

There are at least two versions of this painting, one in the Tate Gallery and another in the Fitzwilliam Museum, Cambridge. The latter has a more serious expression, but either version can be used for the activity. Gwen John was herself a very solitary person, living with her cat and making a series of intense but unsuitable friendships. She made several paintings of girls reading letters, always unsmiling.

Display the painting where the children can study it and ask for their comments. What is the person feeling? Where is she? What does she have with her? Do you think she is enjoying her letter? Is she relaxed in her chair? Do you imagine her to be alone or are there other people in the room? What kind of colours has Gwen John used in the painting? What does the title mean and does it give you clues about her demeanour and location? What do you think the girl's letter says? Is it the letter that has made her sad or was she sad before?

The literacy activity

Ask the children to compose the letter that they think the girl is reading. Is it formal, from a business, school or hospital? Is it informal, from a friend or relative? If formal, the recipient's address should appear on the left as well as the writer's at the top right. Note the date of the painting – 1920. What time of year might it be? Include the date on the letter. In 1920 formal letters might have been written on typewriters and informal with a fountain pen. If it is possible, providing these would add to the visual authenticity of the letters. The letter should also be signed in an appropriate way – 'Yours sincerely' if she is addressed by name, 'Yours faithfully' if she is not (e.g. Dear Pupil, Dear Madam) or a less formal ending if from a friend.

You could then ask the children what letter they would like to send to her, given her circumstances. Children can then write their own personal letters to the girl.

Further ideas (Reception–Year 6)

Becoming the painting   Ask children to put themselves in the girl's shoes – try sitting in the same way, and miming drinking her tea or opening and then reading the letter in the way they feel the girl would. Create the picture by asking an appropriate child to pose with props.

If you could visit her, what would you say to the girl in the picture? (If the mood is sufficiently sensitive, children could take turns to speak to the child representing the girl in the picture.) Has anyone ever helped you by talking or by sending a letter?

Chapter 2

Materials

We are surrounded by materials which are necessary to our lives. Exploring their different properties, behaviour, appearance and texture helps children to understand what can be expected of each and how the correct choice of material is essential when considering design and function. Discovering the origins of materials increases understanding of the earth and offers wide scope for further exploration in science, art, geography and history.

Drama

'Auntie's Object'

A light-hearted storyline is used to increase children's understanding of where materials come from and how they are obtained.

Suitable for   Whole class, Reception to Year 6. The level of detail and knowledge can be adjusted according to age and ability.

You will need   An object which is made from at least three materials. For the 'Auntie' storyline to work well it is best to choose something old or unusual, such as an Edwardian wooden toy with rubber wheels and a string, an old teddy made of cloth and sawdust with glass eyes, or a 1920s beaded bag with metal clasp. I use my grandmother's diabolo set, which is made of wood, metal and cotton. If such items are hard to obtain you can use a modern table lamp, shoe, paintbrush, etc. and miss out the story of auntie, which relies on her valuing an old or rare object. Auntie can, of course, become uncle, grandmother/father or any other friend or relative – even the local museum!

Introduction

Stand to indicate that the drama has begun (see Notes on Drama, p. 1) and show the chosen object. Explain that it belongs to your auntie and that she very kindly lent it to you to bring to school for our project on materials. Discuss with the children what materials it is made from. The trouble is, there's a problem. Auntie owns two of these, each identical to the other. They are very precious to her because one was her mother's and the other belonged to her mother's twin sister when they were little girls. She lent you both of them. They are old and are not made any more. And you have lost one. You have turned the house upside down and it is simply not there. You think the neighbour's dog may have run off with it. (You can elaborate on this – you have put up notices asking if anyone has seen it and had no reply, etc. The important thing to establish is that it cannot be found and an identical one cannot be bought.) Auntie will be extremely upset if she finds out. The only thing to do is to make one exactly like it.

The drama

The aim of the drama is to help children to understand that the making of one object from several materials may involve many people, locations and expertise, and that materials come from specific sources, often in specific parts of the world. As teacher, you need to do research on how and from where the three materials in your object are obtained. For young children the knowledge imparted through the drama can be basic, while for older Key Stage 2 pupils the drama can take the form of an accurate and serious simulation, and may cover more than one session.

Whatever their age, ask the children which part of the object they think should be made first, and where this material comes from. This drama gives good opportunities to incorporate any knowledge the children may already have. For example, a child's parent may be a carpenter or a sheet metal worker and the child may know something of the process of their work.

Your drama journey may include travelling to a rubber plantation in Malaysia and making a mould of the original rubber parts of the object, visiting a forest of the correct wood type and learning to fell a tree safely and operate a log-cutting machine (wearing the right safety gear), tin mining, picking cotton in America, or harvesting clay with a mechanical digger and taking it to the factory to be cleaned and processed in a pugging mill. As a team you will need to discuss the finer points of copying the object – how to get the exact shape, which tools to use, how to make it look as old and worn as the original.

There are various ways to bring the storyline to a close. You could post the two items back to auntie and then telephone her to ask if they have arrived safely, crossing your fingers in front of the children as you dial. 'Hello? Oh, good, you got my parcel. Was everything all right?' (bated breath, then huge thumbs up sign to the children) 'Yes, I'm sure you're glad to see them again – they were very useful to us . . .', etc. Or you could arrive home and find that the neighbour's dog had returned the missing object, or that it had been found by a member of the public. Sit down to signify the end of the drama.

It is important, when the drama has finished, to end the session by pointing out that the experience included an imaginary auntie and an imaginary situation, and discussing what we should actually do if ever we lost something belonging to another person. Other parts of the drama experience, though, are based on reality, and you can point out that there are people right now, all over the world, working to gather, grow or dig raw materials to make the objects of tomorrow.

Further ideas (Key Stage 1)

Blow your house down For Key Stage 1, your drama can revolve around testing the story of the three little pigs, and can include the following activities: growing some corn, cutting it down, making straw, building a house; cutting sticks in a forest and building a second house; making bricks from clay and firing them for the third house. Test each house by getting the whole class to blow on them. The drama is helped by children having a clear idea of the materials beforehand – let them handle some straw and sticks and look at a brick wall, observing the way the bricks are placed and the mortar between them.

See also Paintings – Drama (Key Stages 1 and 2) and History – Drama (Key Stage 2) for further ideas on materials.

Dance

The properties of wood

A dance about where wood comes from, its use and the effect fire has on wood.

Suitable for   Whole class, Reception to Year 6 – the dance has a simple storyline but different levels of sophistication in the movements that can be achieved according to the age and ability of the children.

You will need   Choreographed music: 'Prelude'/'Fire World' from *Fire and Ice* by Carl Davis. The whole of this work is very useful for the theme of Materials, offering contrasts in the worlds of ice and fire and what happens when the two meet. Suggested alternative music: The mood should be quiet at the beginning and become more restless, building to a climax and fading away. Benjamin Britten's *Four Sea Interludes* (No. 1, 'Dawn') and Grieg's 'In the Hall of the Mountain King' from his *Peer Gynt Suite* both contain the necessary changes of mood, as do many other orchestral pieces.

Introduction

Discuss fire – the shape of flames and how they move, how a fire is started and how and why it spreads. What materials catch fire easily? Introduce vocabulary such as 'combustible', 'flammable'. Talk about wood and what effect fire has on it. The effect can be good (we can light a wood fire to warm ourselves or to cook on) or it can be bad, as in a forest fire. Our dance aims to show both effects.

The dance

Before beginning, choose three to six children to be 'the picnic group'. This group has more of a miming/acting role than a dancing one, which may help when selecting.

0.00   The music begins with a quiet, peaceful introduction. Dancers can begin curled up as small seeds on the earth, spread over the working area but with a space in the middle – this will become the picnic site. During the introduction the seeds grow, stretch, reach for the light and develop into trees. The hackneyed image of children standing with arms stuck in the air at the suggestion, 'Let's all be trees' should be firmly banned here! Encourage children to see themselves not as individual trees but as one forest. Dance requires good teamwork – ask the children to be aware of the other dancers, adopting different shapes from others, checking at all times that their own body shape is interesting or unusual, and that there is a balance in the forest – some trees gnarled and stunted, others tall and graceful, some branches or trunks twisted, roots spreading out, etc. Gently stir in the breeze.

0.36   The trees have grown and the picnic group enters slowly, looking around at the beauty and stillness of the forest. In mime they discuss and point to possible sites and choose the space in the middle, spreading out a rug, unpacking a hamper, etc.

0.57   At the menacing change in the music the picnickers move around the forest snapping or chopping off branches from the trees to make a fire. When a tree is selected for this it should react accordingly – as the arm is held and the snapping movement is made by the picnicker, the child playing the tree should drop the arm and hold it next to the body so that it appears to have been chopped off. The picnickers mime carrying the branches to the picnic space in the centre.

1.30 A theme tune begins and the picnickers gather round the pile of branches while one mimes holding up two sticks and rubs them together, gradually blowing on them to make a flame, which is then dropped on the branches. The picnickers warm their hands at the flame, eat and wander off to explore (exit from work space.)

1.55 A flute theme begins. The picnickers have carelessly left their fire and a spark has caught the nearest tree. Choose which child will be the tree that first catches fire. This child begins by flickering the fingers only. All other dancers must watch carefully as the flicker passes around, spreading through the forest. Eventually all trees are flickering. The music builds up and the flickering spreads to include hands, wrists, arms and upper body.

2.17 The music builds into a powerful and loud version of the theme. At this point the trees can uproot themselves and become fierce flames, whirling, leaping and diving. Use any abilities children may have – cartwheels, handstands, etc. can add greatly to the visual impact. Care must be taken to avoid bumping – teach children always to seek and move into a space.

2.43 Trumpets sound. The picnickers return and look with horror at the scene. They rip off their coats and beat the flames. Some grab their food containers and run to the river for water.

3.15 The climax of the music arrives, and the picnickers throw water over the flames, which gradually die down, melting to the ground as the music fades (a sizzling sound can be heard in the music.) All is still and the picnickers are left panting and staring at the burnt forest.

3.36 Fade and turn off the music.

Further ideas (Years 3–6)

Extending the dance   The music continues at 3.36 for a further loud and then fading section after the above. Older children could discuss ideas for incorporating this final section into the dance. Perhaps a machine is brought into the forest to clear up the mess. One idea for the final fading of the piece (which ends with a faint crackling sound) is for a child to wander into the middle with a piece of paper, pretend to pick up a piece of wood from the burnt remains of the forest, and mime writing on the paper, which could then be laid on the floor to reveal the previously prepared charcoal message 'DO NOT START FIRES'.

Art

Wax and ice sculptures

An exciting activity in which two contrasting materials are used to make small but striking sculptures.

Suitable for   Small group at a time, Key Stage 1 should not pour wax; Key Stage 2 children will be able to pour their own wax with supervision.

You will need   Ice cubes, about 6–8 per sculpture (polythene ice cube bags are ideal – fill as many as you need the day before and freeze overnight); batik or candle wax; wax crayons of different colours; safe containers for melting wax, from which the wax can also be poured, such as metal pans with pouring lips; newspaper; scissors; plastic yogurt or cream pots (one per sculpture); old teaspoons or lolly sticks; use of stove and sink. A fire blanket or wet tea towel should be to hand.

Introduction

Show the children a cube of ice and a piece of wax. What do these materials have in common? They are both solids, and both melt when heat is applied. However, wax will become solid again at room temperature, whereas water needs to be frozen to turn it back into ice. We are going to see how the two materials react when put together. Warn the children about the danger of hot pans.

The art activity

Put a safe amount of candle or batik wax into each pan – when melted the wax should only reach halfway up the pan. Add a wax crayon or two to each pan so that each contains a different colour. Heat the pans very gently on the stove, watching them at all times. The wax should never bubble or smoke, although it will steam a little. (Not only is over-hot wax dangerous, but it will also melt the yogurt pots, distorting the sculptures.) Spread newspaper on a suitable surface as near to the stove as possible and stand the yogurt pots on it (it is a good idea to name one for each child first.)

When one pan of wax is liquid, stir with a lolly stick or old teaspoon to ensure even distribution of colour. Children who want this colour for their sculpture should now fill their yogurt pot with ice as fully as possible. It does not matter if the ice protrudes from the top of the pot. Ice can be crushed, but avoid using pieces which are smaller than a marble as they either melt too quickly or get lost inside the sculpture. An adult, or an older child under adult supervision, should now pour the wax directly into the yogurt pot over the ice, stopping just short of the top. Continue until all pots are filled with ice and the chosen colour of wax.

The pots should not be touched for at least 5 minutes, but there is important value in observing them during this time to note the changes that are taking place. Which material do the children consider reacts more quickly to the other? Does the ice melt before the wax hardens, or vice versa? After 5 minutes gently shake a pot. Sometimes ice can be heard still rattling inside it. If so, leave the pots for longer.

Let each child carefully invert their pot over a sink and release the water which used to be ice. Make a snip in the top edge of each pot with scissors and help the children to peel the pot carefully away, revealing the sculpture. These can be very delicate, so handle with care. Stand the sculptures on newspaper to drain thoroughly before displaying.

Further ideas (Reception–Year 6)

Bi-coloured sculptures   After pouring out the water from the sculpture, pour a contrasting coloured wax into the holes made by the ice. Do not peel the pot away until it feels completely cold.

Candle sculptures   Hold a length of wick vertically in the pot before dropping the ice cubes around it to secure it. Pour in wax. Your ice sculpture will now be a candle.

Sand sculptures   Pour a jug or two of water into a deep tray of play sand to make it damp and firm. Let children press objects such as shells, the bottom of an apple or a finger into the sand and remove carefully. Pour wax into the holes and allow to set. Children love to dig out the resulting sculptures, which can be washed under a tap. Wicks can also be inserted before pouring the wax.

Literacy

Six-adjective poems

A simple poetry formula to encourage use of descriptive words.

Suitable for   Reception to Year 6, as a class, in groups or individually according to ability.

You will need   Paper, pencils, whiteboard and marker.

Introduction

Ask the class to choose one material that they have studied. When a consensus is reached, write the name of the chosen material (for example, 'ice') at the bottom of the whiteboard.

The literacy activity

Ask the class to suggest words which describe the material. These must be single adjectives only, not phrases such as 'melts in the heat'. A good way to do this is to work through the senses ('what does it look/sound/feel/smell/taste like?') and then 'how does it behave?' Write as many as possible down both sides of the whiteboard. Suggestions might include 'hard', 'frozen', 'sparkly', 'glittering', 'slippery', 'cold', 'transparent', etc., according to the age of the children.

When a large number of words has been collected, explain that we need only six of them for our poem. Encourage children to be discerning about the words they choose. Which tell us most about the material? Do some mean the same as others? Are some more accurate? Which are the most unusual, imaginative or sound most interesting? Gradually begin to cross off those words which are weaker than others. For example, children might reject 'cold' as being too ordinary and not as accurate as 'frozen', or 'slidy' because it had a similar meaning to 'slippery'.

When the collection is whittled down to six, let the class discuss the order in which they should be placed for best effect. Some words might go together well because they are alliterative, such as 'slippery' and 'slidy'. Some words might have a rhythm which sounds good in a certain position. When a decision is reached, write the six adjectives in the chosen order above the word you wrote at the bottom of the whiteboard. A Key Stage 2 finished poem might read:

    sparkling
    splintered
    frostbitten
    fragile
    glassy
    untrustworthy
    ice

A Key Stage 1 version might be:

    smooth
    grainy
    brown
    barky
    strong
    useful
    wood

Whichever words are used, the result is a simple poem with a pleasing rhythm. Having worked on the first poem as a class, children can now work individually, or in groups with adult help, to produce six-adjective poems about other materials.

Further Ideas (Years 2–6)

Choral speaking   Bring the poems to life by asking the class to read them aloud, using appropriate voice levels and sound effects (e.g. a woodblock for a poem on wood).

Viewpoint poems   How is the material viewed by others?

> The Eskimo looked at the ice cube and saw . . . (a home)
> The ant looked at the ice cube and saw . . . (a skating rink)
> The nurse looked at the ice cube and saw . . . (a relief for a sprained ankle)

Chapter 3

History

'The past is a foreign country: they do things differently there', says L. P. Hartley in the opening line of his novel *The Go-Between*. So what is the best way to learn about a foreign country? Ideally it is to go there – no amount of reading, watching films or talking to natives can ever take the place of actual experience. Children cannot actually visit the foreign country of the past, but drama can offer them experiences so close to reality that it is the ideal teaching method through which to approach history.

Drama

'Teddy's Time Machine'

This drama is designed to help young children learn about past and present toys and the differences between them, and to grasp the concept of time passing and words such as 'past', 'present' and 'future'. It incorporates the use of actual artefacts so that it can be followed up with work such as drawing and writing in the classroom.

Suitable for   Whole class, Reception, Years 1 and 2, possibly some older children.

You will need   A teddy bear or similar toy with character (i.e. not a top or a ball), as old as possible; a selection of toys of the same era (probably Victorian or Edwardian), enough for one toy per group of 4–5 children, and an old-looking suitcase or box to hold them; similar selection of modern toys, as contrasting with the old toys as possible (plastic, batteries, moving parts, etc.) and a modern container for them; paper and a pencil; music to evoke time travel which can be switched on and off easily by the teacher. The old suitcase and the new container should be placed in the workspace prior to the lesson, preferably somewhere not too obvious, or covered with a cloth.

Introduction

Gather the children and introduce the teddy (or other toy). Ask them if they think he is old or new, and how they can tell. After this, tell the children that Teddy is feeling sad. He is many, many years old and used to belong to a boy in a Victorian house with a nursery upstairs (if the actual history of the toy is known, this can be used). He remembers the old suitcase/toy box where he used to be kept with his other toy friends, and he misses them very much. There is only one way he will ever be able to see them again, but that is impossible, because he doesn't know anyone who could help him.

Hopefully the children will ask what the way is, and if they can help! Hold Teddy to your ear and tell the children that he says he has heard that the only way to go back in time is to build a time machine.

The drama

Put Teddy where he can watch the children, and ask them how the time machine should be made. What will it need? Use as many of the children's ideas as possible. To make it look official (and to aid your memory) you might want to write them down. Encourage the children to think of the practical side of making the machine as well as the imaginative. Suggestions received from Reception and Year 1 children have included: making enough seats for everybody, plus a little one at the front for teddy; powerful brakes to stop at the right year; a starter button; seat-belts; a large clock face like a propeller 'with years instead of hours'; and big windows so we could see the years changing as we went by. The children all agreed that the machine should fly, and have a very big petrol tank so that there was no danger of us being stuck in the wrong year.

Once the design has been agreed divide the children into groups of 4 to 5 and designate the work – seats, doors, tank, clock, etc. Keep the atmosphere busy but controlled. What materials does each group need and where will they get them? Have they thought how to fasten the parts together safely? Pretend to give some money and directions to a scrapyard or DIY store. Make a call on an imaginary mobile phone to locate certain parts you may need. Are the seats padded in case of sudden stops? Do they have seat-belts? Are the door locks secure?

Announce that it is time to assemble the parts, asking children to drag or carry them to the centre of the workspace. Everyone works to fix them together. Choose a driver and place Teddy in his seat. Strap yourselves in and shut the doors. You can then switch on the time machine music and travel through time to the selected year. You could describe the changing scene as you go back in time, 'Look at the old-fashioned cars! Oh, now there are hardly any cars at all. Look at the horses and carriages!'. Or you could count backwards through the years, '1990, 1980, 1970, 1960 . . .' and follow this up later with a timeline in the classroom.

Stop the time machine in the chosen year and get out rather warily. How wrong your clothes look compared to those of the people walking by! How different the sounds are – street cries, a distant barrel organ, no aeroplanes overhead, the clopping of horses. Ask Teddy to direct you to the house where he first lived. Here it is – it's tall, with railings and steps up to a front door. You pull a bell handle and a maid lets you in. Creep up the stairs, then up the stairs again. Teddy says, 'This is the nursery'. And there in the corner is the suitcase he remembers.

You can now put the children in their groups again and give one toy from the case to each group. Carry Teddy round to each group – any queries the children may have about their toy can be answered through him. If time permits, allow groups to change to a different toy; if not, they can be studied later in the classroom.

Put the toys back in the suitcase, gather the children together and explain that although Teddy has had a wonderful time with his old toy friends he is still rather sad, because now he is missing his current owner and house. Teddy is too old to be played with, and his owner is a grown-up who keeps him on a shelf. But the owner has a son and a daughter who play with toys. The only trouble is that Teddy does not understand modern toys or how they work.

Play the music as you travel back in the time machine, counting up to the present year. Teddy leads the children to his present home and the modern toys are shared between groups as before. This time, when you take Teddy round to each group, the children explain and demonstrate the toys to him.

To end the session gather the children together so that Teddy can thank them for building the machine.

Further ideas (Key Stage 2)

See also Machines – Drama, about Victorian fairgrounds.

Tips for historical drama   There are many ways to explore history through drama. As with the above lesson, the best approach is to devise a task which the children must carry out as a team, and to incorporate into the drama as many accurate facts about the period as possible, which you as teacher will need to research beforehand.

Warning: Always choose a manageable task which involves working and discussing together. Never try to act out a disaster such as a battle, sinking of the Mary Rose, blowing up of Houses of Parliament, etc. This has the potential to deteriorate into mayhem and very little learning takes place. It is far more valuable to enact the events leading up to or immediately following the disaster.

The following are suggestions for Key Stage 2 children:

Ancient Greece   The class takes on the role of Athenian carpenters. A scroll is delivered commanding them to fashion a huge horse of wood in total secrecy. It is signed by the king, Odysseus. How will they hide it? When and where will they build it? What tools and materials will they use? How will they deliver it?

Tudors   King Henry VIII is holding a great banquet (class can decide on a historical reason for this.) Allow children to see two different sides of the event by first becoming the guests, practising their dancing, touring the rooms and being dressed for the occasion, and then the servants, preparing the fires, making candles, turning the spit, baking, scrubbing, cooking, going to the icehouse, etc.

Vikings   You have arrived by ship in England. Establish a settlement of longhouses showing the younger members of your community how to mark them out and build them, selecting suitable wood and using tools they have made. Prepare and hold a feast to thank the gods for your safe journey and new home. What clothes will you make for the occasion and how long would they take to plan and prepare?

For fuller details of these and other history-based dramas and dances, see the author's Creative History Activity Packs (Suggested Further Reading).

Dance

Prometheus and Pandora

This dance depicts the legend of Prometheus and Pandora's box, and sets it to one of the few remaining pieces of ancient Greek music to have miraculously survived. The episode of Prometheus being chained to a rock and his liver eaten out has been omitted from the dance, but add it if you wish!

Suitable for   Whole class, Key Stage 2.

You will need   The story of Prometheus and Pandora (to read or tell.) Choreographed music: Track 8, *Hymne à Nemesis*, from *Musique de la Grèce Antique*, HMA 1951015. You will need to use this twice in succession as it is rather short. Suggested alternative music: Any music that is proud and stirring, reflecting the power of the gods, or builds to a climax as the story unfolds. The *Fire and Ice* piece by Carl Davis used for the dance in the Materials chapter provides a suitable atmosphere for the storyline. Berlioz's *The Trojans* has a powerful marching rhythm, while Saint-Saens' *Danse Macabre*, Grieg's 'In the Hall of the Mountain King' from the *Peer Gynt Suite* and Paul Dukas's *The Sorcerer's Apprentice* are perfect for the Pandora's Box theme.

Introduction

Read or tell to the class the story of Prometheus stealing fire from Heaven, and Pandora's box. Explain that the Ancient Greeks were skilled storytellers, dancers and actors, and that live entertainment was a vital part of their culture, and was so admirable that their plays are still acted and their stories still told today. We know that dance was also of great importance to the Ancient Greeks because of the number of pots which are decorated with images of dancers. Sadly, there is no remaining record of their choreography, so little is known of the actual steps. Similarly, only fragments of written music still exist.

The dance

Choose children to represent Zeus (a powerful role with not much movement), Prometheus, Epimetheus (these two roles require mime rather than dancing), Man, Pandora (these two children can join in the dance with the class until their roles begin.)

The piece begins with four drum beats and a drone. These sounds represent Zeus. The rest of the piece is composed of five easily recognisable four-line stanzas, so when played twice through will give you ten stanzas.

0.00   On the drums and drone Zeus takes up a powerful attitude towards the back of the working space and in the middle.

0.09   (1st stanza) All other children take up positions as Titans on either side of him, bowing in worship. Epimetheus can be positioned at one side of Zeus and Prometheus at the other. Zeus motions Epimetheus to step forward.

Figure 3 The animals show their gifts

0.25 (2nd and 3rd stanzas) Titans move forward into the working space and form groups, now representing animals. You could have eight groups as there are eight lines of music in the two stanzas. On each line of music Epimetheus points to a group of animals and gives them a gift, such as strength, speed, camouflage, beauty, wings, claws, shells, horns. Children can decide which animals and gifts are to be represented. As each group is given its gift they show it in movement by moving to the edge of the working space to form a semi-circle opposite Zeus. The children playing Man and Pandora need to make sure that they are positioned nearest Zeus, one at each end of the semi-circle. These two children lie down and keep very still. Epimetheus steps back to his place at Zeus's side.

0.56 (4th stanza) Prometheus flies down from Heaven (perhaps round the work space in a circle rather than directly) to the child playing Man. He mimes making Man from clay, sitting him up, and finally standing him up, a living creature. The animals can react to this, and likewise to the events in the next stanza.

1.12 (5th stanza) Prometheus flies back to Heaven in a circle, and cautiously approaches the sun, which is represented by several children who move forward from the animal line as he flies, and form a round cluster in the centre, flickering their hands to imitate flames. Prometheus puts his hand into the sun, and as he withdraws it, makes it flicker also, to show that he has stolen some fire. He holds his flickering hand above his head and flies down to earth. He presents the fire to the Man (as he passes it over, he stops his hand flickering and the Man's hand flickers instead) and they both move to join the main semi-circle. Here the piece ends and needs to be repeated for the rest of the dance.

0.00 (6th stanza) The drums and drone signal Zeus again. He is very angry at what Prometheus has done. He moves to where Pandora is lying at the ends of the semi-circle. He mimes making a woman, Pandora, from clay in the same way that Prometheus formed the man.

0.25 (7th stanza) Epimetheus stares at Pandora and moves towards her. They stare at each other. They are in love. Zeus and the animals can react to this, perhaps with satisfied smiles and nods, or rolled eyes and shaking of the head. Epimetheus leads Pandora to his home. While Pandora looks around, all the other children (except Zeus and Epimetheus) move into the centre of the space and crowd low and close together to represent the closed box.

0.40 (8th stanza) Epimetheus is still showing Pandora around his home. He leads her to the box. She looks interested and moves towards it but he stops her, warning her in mime never to open it. He then leaves, maybe blowing her a kiss.

0.56 (9th and 10th stanzas) Pandora cannot resist. She moves towards the box and flings open the lid. (It is important that a large, clear movement is used for this – not only is it more dramatic, but it is the cue for the other dancers to leave the box. Two imaginary central handles, flung apart like a huge book, is effective.) All the characteristics that Epimetheus chose not to give the animals pour out. Children can decide how to use their bodies and faces to represent disease, envy, spite, revenge, hatred, greed, etc. Use all the music up to 1.27 to fill the room with whirling, evil shapes gradually escaping from the box until only one child remains in it to represent Hope.

1.27 Pandora collapses on the floor in horror.

1.31 To end the dance, Hope flies out and circles Pandora, who runs after her. As they exit and the drone dies away only Zeus remains, watching from his place of power.

Further ideas (Key Stage 2)

Three possible approaches to addressing history through dance are:

1   To teach authentic historical dances, such as Tudor, Victorian, etc., using authentic music.
2   To enact a story or event from history through dance (as in the example above.)
3   To take movements from everyday activities or events of the period and build them into a dance. For example, an alternative Ancient Greek dance could incorporate movements inspired by a potter's wheel, carpentry, bread making, fishing, use of weapons, reclining to eat, statues, the Olympic games, comedy and tragedy in the theatre.

Art

Dyeing with plants

This fascinating activity, which I have carried out numerous times with children of all ages, complements the study of people from many historical periods, including Ancient Greeks, Romans, Vikings, Saxons and Tudors, all of whom used plants to dye cloth and wool. Results are achieved quickly, and children can experiment to recreate some of the colours which would have been familiar to people of the past, and use their dyed pieces in various ways.

Suitable for   Small group (maximum six), Reception to Year 6, with constant adult supervision.

You will need   Use of a stove or one/two-ring hotplate; plenty of newspaper; old pans with heatproof handles (not used for food); dyestuffs (list follows); cream of tartar/alum (see dyestuffs list); sticks or wooden spoons; natural white or cream-coloured wool (no nylon or synthetic content) and/or pieces of sheep's fleece; strips of pure cotton cloth (no polyester content); old pairs of tights cut into 15 cm lengths; indelible laundry pen or ballpoint; large jug of water; washing up bowl or bucket; damp towel or fire blanket nearby.

Dye stuffs can include those easily bought, gathered or found in the kitchen: onion skins, tea, coffee, clover, dandelion, chamomile, parsley, rose petals, turmeric, henna, elderberries, blackberries, red cabbage or any other plant you want to try. Or you can buy more unusual ready prepared dried plant dyes as well as more common plants (suppliers' details are at the end of this section.) Alum, a mordant which prepares the wool to receive the dyes and enhances their colours, can also be obtained from the supplier listed, or can sometimes be ordered from pharmacies. Cream of tartar does the same job but with different colour results, so it is exciting to compare the two.

Introduction

Plants have been used for centuries in many different parts of the world to alter the colour of wool or cloth to be used for clothes. Some dyes, such as broom and woad, were common, while others, because of their rarity, came to be associated with the wealthy. Before beginning, it is important that children understand that:

1   They will be working with hot water and a stove, so calm behaviour and obeying of instructions is essential.
2   The dyes, and fingers which have handled them, should not be put in the mouth (though none of the dyestuffs listed above is toxic).
3   The work is experimental; there may be disappointments as well as exciting results.

The procedure, like cooking, is perfectly safe if some obvious rules are observed:

Flexes or extension leads must be taped to the floor.
The pan handle should always be held firmly while the contents are being stirred.
Only one person at a time to each pan.
No pushing or hurrying.
The adult must be present at the stove at all times.
Children who are not doing the activity must keep away from the area.

If you are using pieces of sheep's fleece to dye, children can wash these in warm water with a little washing up liquid. If the fleece is left dirty, the grease in it will prevent the dye from penetrating. You can also try washing it in soapwort (see end of section for supplier) which was the plant used for cleansing in past times.

A mordant is not essential but sometimes results can be disappointing without one. There are several types, but alum and cream of tartar are safe for children to use. In past generations (right up to Victorian times) the most common mordant was urine!

The art activity

If you are using mordant, children can place a tablespoonful in a pan with the items which are to be dyed; either lengths of wool (the length will depend on what you want to use it for later – if you intend to sew or weave with it, use up to a metre per child per dye; if you simply wish to see a colour on it, short lengths will do), pieces of washed sheep's fleece, or strips of cotton cloth. Add just enough water from the jug to barely cover the materials. (You may need to mordant a couple of pansful for each group if every child wants to try every dye.) Bring to the boil, and holding pan handle firmly, children can take turns to stir with a stick or wooden spoon for about a minute. The adult should then pour the water into the bucket or washing up bowl and place wool/cotton on thick newspaper. Allow to cool and squeeze out.

To dye the materials, pour about 1.5 cm depth of water from the jug into the pans. Using more will weaken the colour of the dyes. Tie a knot in the end of a cut length from the tights to form a bag. Put your chosen plant dye into the bag – try a heaped teaspoonful if the plant is dried and a good handful if the plant is fresh – and tie up the open end. Put one dye bag in each pan.

If you wish, you can tie a label showing the child's name and the plant and mordant used on each item by using ballpoint or indelible pen on a cotton strip.

Choose one child per pan (children can take turns, but only one child per pan at a time). Place the pan on the ring, which should be turned to its highest setting. The child should hold the pan handle firmly with one hand and have the stick or spoon in the other, but should not stir until the water actually boils. When it does so, the bag of dye should be gently poked to encourage the colour to seep out. The child should continue kneading the bag gently with the stick or spoon until the wool or cotton changes colour. Do not turn down the heat.

If a colour change is going to happen, it will occur in about one minute. If, after this time, nothing has happened or you have a disappointing result, abandon it and try another dye. Remove the dye bag with the stick and discard in the bucket or washing up bowl. Fish out the dyed items and place on a thick pad of newspaper to drain and cool. Empty the water from the pan into the bucket also.

While some children are stirring, others can be preparing the next bags of dye and pieces of wool, so that a smooth system is achieved.

When cool enough to handle and not too drippy, the dyed items may be hung in a convenient place to dry thoroughly before being used for display, weaving, plaiting or stitching.

Further ideas (Years 2–6)

Experiments

1   Try different amounts of dye.
2   Try different amounts of water. (Older children can weigh and measure dyes and water and keep accurate recordings.)
3   Try the same plant in fresh and dried form.
4   Try dyeing materials other than wool and cotton.
5   Try the dyes with and without mordant.

These experiments provide valuable links with Science and Design Technology.

Display

1   Wrap wools as neatly as possible around a small stiff piece of card and display in a book or on the wall.
2   Show the process in your display by mounting an unwashed piece of sheep's wool, a washed piece, mordanted pieces and dyed pieces in a sequence.
3   Display in baskets on a surface: one basket of sheep's fleece, one of plant dyes and one of a collection of dyed wools.

Recommended suppliers

Fibrecrafts, Old Portsmouth Road, Peasmarsh, Guildford, Surrey GU3 1LZ.
01483 565800 <sales@fibrecrafts.co.uk> or <sales@georgeweil.co.uk>
Wide selection of wools and fleeces, dried plant dyes, mordants, equipment, books, plus advice.

Midland Herbs and Spices, 1a Forman's Trading Estate, Pentos Drive, Sparkhill, Birmingham B11 3TA. 0121 778 5771 <midland.herbs@virgin.net>
Soapwort for washing fleece.

Literacy

Guy Fawkes' diary

A diary is the most private form of writing there is, and is unique in that it is often meant never to be seen. It therefore carries a certain excitement when read; a feeling of trespassing. Asking children to write a character's diary is a useful way of helping them consolidate a historical event, and offers them the opportunity not only to record authentic fact but also to add the feelings they imagine the writer would have had. The example given here is the diary of Guy Fawkes, but the idea can be applied to any character, real or imaginary.

Suitable for   Group or class, Years 3–6, although younger children can dictate their ideas to an adult.

You will need   Photocopies of diary pages, showing the relevant date for your project (a photocopiable example is given here); writing tools. For an authentic 'parchment' look, first wipe the paper with damp teabags and allow to dry. Older children can try writing with quill pens dipped in ink.

November 7th 1605

Figure 4 A page from Guy Fawkes' diary

Introduction

Writing someone's diary requires as much knowledge as possible about the person and the times in which he/she lived, so this activity is designed to consolidate rather than launch a project (although an intriguing diary entry, previously prepared by the teacher and read to the class, can provide an exciting stimulus to begin study of a historical period.) So before undertaking this activity ensure that children have enough information to write an informed entry.

Talk to children about the kind of writing a diary might contain. How would it differ from other kinds of writing, such as letters or newspaper reports? Why do people write them? For whom is a diary written? How can diaries be useful in the study of history? If possible, show or read children examples from actual published diaries of the past such as those of Anne Hughes (1796–1797), Thomas Turner (1754–1765) or Parson James Woodforde (1758–1802)

The literacy activity

Equip children with the diary page and writing tool (see *You will need*, above). If the pages are to be displayed, the entries can of course be written in rough first. Draw attention to the date on the diary page. (4 November 1605 was the day that Lord Mounteagle came to inspect the cellar under the Houses of Parliament where two tons of gunpowder were stored, hidden under firewood. Mounteagle pretended to have seen only the wood, but the next day soldiers were waiting for Fawkes.)

Discuss the time of day, or night, when Guy Fawkes would be writing the entry. Late that night? A few days later? Maybe the events of the day would have a bearing on when he had time to write it. If he wrote it several days after the events, how would his entry differ from a diary entry he might have written immediately? (He might have forgotten, or remembered, details, realised something in hindsight, formed opinions or regrets, seen the consequences of his actions.)

He might also record other facts or thoughts which had no bearing on the historic plot, or were influenced by it. (Parson Woodforde, for example, faithfully recorded the weather and what he ate every day of his life, though it is unlikely that Guy Fawkes would be concerned with such things on the date in question!) Use historical evidence to supply further possibilities. Perhaps Fawkes was worried about his family members, or was reminiscing about his days in York, or worrying about his rent for the cellar. Encourage children to get inside the character and 'live him from within', so that the diary entry is believable and human while also as historically accurate as possible.

Further ideas (Years 3–6)

Anonymous letter   The conspirators in the Gunpowder Plot included Francis Tresham. His brother-in-law was Lord Mounteagle, whom Tresham knew would be in the Houses of Parliament when they were due to explode. To protect him, Tresham sent him an anonymous warning letter. Ask children to write this letter. How would you phrase it to make sure it was taken seriously but without revealing the identity of the writer?

Non-violent answers   The conspirators took their drastic action because they felt they were being treated unfairly. Discuss with the children times when they have felt like this/been very angry. What other methods could the conspirators have used to make changes? What things would you like to change in school/where you live/in the world? How could you make these changes without resorting to violence? Sometimes the answer is to write a letter to a person who has the power or responsibility to deal with the situation, such as a teacher, councillor or MP. Ask children to draft a letter on a matter they would like to change.

Be a reporter   Write a newspaper report of the Gunpowder Plot. Choose a suitable date and headlines. The headlines may differ according to the view expressed by the newspaper. Help children to recognise the important points and to cut out the extraneous material.

Chapter 4

Journeys

Everyone makes journeys. They can be physical journeys, ranging from a daily car trip to a major exploration, emotional journeys, pleasant or painful, or spiritual journeys, in which the mind travels to new places and levels of understanding. Some journeys are so important that they are life-changing, or so famous that they have become part of history. But all journeys are very personal, and this chapter offers opportunities for children to explore their own journeys, those of others and those of the imagination.

Drama

A magic carpet ride

A magic carpet makes an ideal imaginary vehicle to carry you on a journey in a drama session. The ideas below can be adapted to travel on any journey you wish.

Suitable for Whole class, Reception–Year 3.

You will need A simple booklet with chosen destinations and spells to make the carpet rise and descend (full details below); tape of suitable 'flying' music (something quiet and mysterious) – I use 'An Ending (Ascent)' by Eno, on *Classical Chillout 2*, 7234 5 62087 2 8 VTDCD 437.

The Booklet: an interesting visual aid makes a good focus for starting a piece of drama. The booklet used for the magic carpet ride gives structure to the drama and can be used afterwards to consolidate the work and as a souvenir of the journey. It should be of intriguing appearance (I made mine from circular navy blue paper with silver writing) with one page for each destination you want to visit and a front cover. You can, of course visit only one destination if there is a particular venue you have been studying with the children, but if you want to visit contrasting places to compare them, I suggest a maximum of three, unless you want the drama to cover more than one session.

On the front cover you can write 'Magic carpet journey'. This allows children to see what these words look like and also verifies that the booklet definitely goes with the carpet. Inside the front cover you can write a spell:

> Rise, rise, up to the skies,
> The carpet lifts, and then it flies!

Write a destination on each of your pages and then on the back cover the spell:

> Carpet, land upon the ground
> So we can take a look around!

Introduction

The magic carpet can be introduced in a number of ways. You could simply say that you dreamt all night of a certain destination and when you woke up there on the floor was a strange, rolled up carpet with a booklet attached, so you have brought it to school just as you found it. (In my lessons the carpet is imaginary and the booklet is real, although you could have a real carpet if you wish, so long as the whole class can fit on it!) Or you could say that you woke and found a mysterious message under your pillow, telling you to go to a carpet shop in town, where something would be waiting for you to collect. In other words, you need to come up with an imaginative way to explain how you came to have the carpet. You can then ask two children to carefully unroll it, and when they have done so, invite all the class to stand round it. This gives them a clear image of the size of the carpet before the journey begins.

The drama

Show the children the front cover of the booklet and ask if any of them can read it. Do they think you should open it? You notice a spell inside the front cover and read it out. Nothing happens. Hopefully children will suggest that it will only work if we all sit on the carpet – if they don't, you will need to make this suggestion!

A common question at this point is how we will get down again. If this occurs, you can 'notice' the spell on the back cover. Although this may be simply part of the storyline for many children, it can act as a comforting reassurance for the more hesitant child for whom the drama seems very real. You can now choose a child to open the booklet at page one and read out the destination. It looks as if the carpet is going to fly us there! What will we need to take? Pack your suitcases – not too much or it may be too heavy for the carpet!

When the children are assembled on the carpet you can all say the rising spell together. Then switch on the music to indicate that the spell is working. You can add to the realism by swaying slightly and encouraging children to look carefully over the side and comment on what they can see. 'There's our school – doesn't it look small?' 'Look – we're flying over London!'

As you near your chosen destination, say the spell on the back cover together and switch off the music as you land. How long you stay at each destination and what you do there is up to you, but have clear aims about what you want the children to learn at each place. Add facts throughout the drama to increase their understanding of the destination, and use any existing knowledge the children may already have as fully as possible.

Repeat the pattern of looking in the booklet for the next destination, packing what you will need, saying the rising spell together, switching on the music, looking down at what you pass on your journey, saying the landing spell and switching off the music, for each destination you visit. This routine is also reassuring for the hesitant child and helps the children remember the storyline later. When all your visits are over, end the lesson by landing back at school and rolling up the carpet.

Further ideas (Reception–Year 6)

Possible destinations for your magic carpet journey might include:

1 a country you have been studying, or two or three contrasting countries;
2 the moon, and/or other planets;
3 the past;
4 an imaginary land where things are done differently;
5 contrasting climates – the Antarctic, a jungle, a desert;
6 locations from books – Hogwarts School, Goldilocks' house, the Hundred Acre Wood.

Journeys and Dance

A tour round Disneyland

When asked where they would most like to go on a journey, one of the most popular answers given by a class of infants was Disneyland. Here a whole day is condensed into one short and simple dance, from the opening of the attractions to the moment they close. The dance can be adapted to represent any theme park or fairground.

Suitable for   Whole class, particularly designed for Reception and Years 1–2, but can be used with older children.

You will need   Visual aids. Children may be able to bring in photographs of themselves pictured on rides or in theme parks. These are useful for children who have not experienced them. Choreographed music: Overture (track 1) from *Barnum* (music by Cy Coleman). Suggested alternative music: Scott Joplin pieces, or anything reminiscent of circuses or fairgrounds; barrel organ music; jolly/noisy/busy atmosphere. A quiet, calm, slow piece of music can be used for the introduction and faded down when the attractions open and the noisy piece begins.

Introduction

Talk with the children about Disneyland or other theme parks they have visited, heard about or seen on television. List as many of the attractions as you can. Discuss how you could represent these attractions with movement. Some may be easier to convey than others. Decide together on five for the dance, each one being represented by a group of children. (The class with whom I first worked on this chose the roller coaster, the mini-train, the teacup roundabout, swimming mermaids in a magical lake, and ghosts from a ghost train.) You will also need two children to be tourists who visit each attraction in turn. These children need to have some acting ability and you can include some speaking if you like.

The dance

Prior to the dance, the children representing the attractions should take up their positions. Each attraction should be in a space of its own and you will need to work out beforehand how and where each is to move to avoid the children bumping into each other. For example, the mini-train might chug up and down one side of the workspace, the teacup roundabout revolve in a corner, the mermaids swim in the middle, etc. Each group needs to decide on its starting position and remain very still in it, as if the machinery is not yet switched on for the day. Faces should be expressionless or heads held down.

0.00   As the quiet introductory music begins, the two tourists enter, perhaps holding hands. They walk hesitantly about, but as yet nothing has come to life. To make the situation clear to an audience, the first child could say, 'None of the rides are open yet' and the second say, 'We're too early.' They exchange disappointed glances as they walk from one ride to another.

0.29   The fast music starts. The two tourists look in excitement at one another and their faces break into beaming smiles as they realise the theme park is opening. The teacher should point at one of the attractions as a signal that it should come to life. (Choose one that will make an impact with its movement, such as a line of children as the roller coaster, rearing high and swooping low around the perimeter of the space.)

0.34, 0.38,	Teacher points to second, third, fourth and fifth attractions to start them in
0.42, 0.46	turn. They should remain absolutely still until brought in. As the attractions whirl around them the two tourists stare in delight and point at the ones they intend to try, miming excited discussion between themselves, jumping up and down and clapping, etc.
0.50	The tourists, together or separately, join each of the attractions in turn. This gives them approximately seven seconds on each one, (**0.50, 0.57, 1.04, 1.11, 1.18**) although it doesn't matter if they don't manage to visit them all. You will need to work out how to incorporate the tourist into each ride. For example, each teacup on the roundabout could be represented by a child revolving with one hand on a hip for the cup handle and the other held out in a curve for the round rim. The tourist could then revolve within this rim.
1.24	The music suddenly ends. The attractions should stop very abruptly and resume their absolutely still starting positions. The tourists, however, are still whirling around excitedly. They gradually stop, panting and realise that the fair is over. They walk together to the middle of the room and look at the stillness around them with disappointed faces. The first can say: 'Ohh . . . it's all closed down.' The second replies 'We've had a lovely time – let's go home.' They walk off together hand in hand.

Tip When representing trains, roller coasters, dragons, snakes or anything which requires a line of children in dance or drama, it is wise not to allow them to hold on to each other. This can cause children to be dragged along or be crushed together, and the line frequently breaks. It is better to choose a leader who can set a manageable pace that can be followed by other children so that the line stays in one cohesive shape. Children's arms are then free to be flung in the air like riders on a roller coaster, chug like the pistons of a train, etc.

Further ideas (Reception–Year 6)

Australia See *Further ideas* under Journeys – Art, page 30.

China Use track 1, 'Chung Kuo', or other tracks from *China* by Vangelis. Motifs might include the Great Wall, bending to gather rice, pagoda roofs, the Terracotta Army, the twelve animals of the Chinese horoscope.

Africa See Feelings – Dance, p. 78.

Magic carpet See Journeys – Drama (page 27). The Disneyland dance and the three further dance ideas mentioned here originally formed part of a performance called 'The Magic Carpet Journey' in which each destination was visited in turn on the magic carpet. The performance ended with the carpet returning to school.

Art

Aboriginal journey prints

The importance to the Aboriginal people of journeys and of recording them was explained to me by an Australian teacher who had taught Aboriginal pupils. The children in my class (Reception, Years 1 and 2) were fascinated by the methods she taught them of recording their own life journeys and moments of significance. I have since found the project to be equally rewarding with Key Stage 2 children and with adults.

Suitable for Whole class or group, Reception–Year 6.

You will need A3 sugar paper in earthy, natural colours such as browns and creams; bottled paint in reddish-brown, black, white and ochre shades; PVA glue; play sand; cotton buds; damp, well squeezed out sponges; examples of Aboriginal art (try the Commonwealth Institute, <www.commonwealth.org.uk> or 020 7603 4535.)

Introduction

When we make journeys, we often record them or mark them in some way. We might write about it in a diary, ask someone to take a photograph of us in a certain place or even scratch our initials somewhere. Explain to the children that, as the Aboriginal people of the past had no cameras, they would often leave the mark of their hand on a rock to record their presence there. This was the equivalent of a portrait and was a very personal sign. They would then decorate the handmark and the surrounding rock with patterns of dots which symbolised journeys. We are now going to record journeys we have made in the ways used by the Aborigines.

The art activity

First, make the handmarks. These are not prints, but stencils. The Aborigines' method was to place their hand on the rock and blow paint made from ground-up rocks from their mouth around the edges to leave the shape of the hand, but this is hardly practical! Instead, show the children how to place their hand on the paper and press around it with a damp sponge dipped in paint. This gives the same stencilled effect, and two or three of these placed in balanced positions on the paper form the basis of the composition.

The handmarks and background can now be decorated with dots. Different patterns of dots carried different meanings – a dot surrounded by a circle of dots meant a dwelling or a home, while a long string of dots represented a physical or spiritual journey. The dots are made by dipping the end of a cotton bud into a thin layer of paint (use a different end for each different colour of paint) and using it as a printing tool. The Aborigines would originally have used sticks, but my Australian colleague assured me that cotton buds are what her modern Aboriginal pupils use! Sand and a little PVA can be added to the paint to give a natural texture.

Encourage the children to think of important landmarks in their lives – places they have lived or moved to, the birth of a sibling or the death of a pet. The teacher needs to be sensitive to any major events or traumas experienced by pupils and should use discretion when undertaking this activity, although it can be a focus in helping children to talk about difficulties and inventing symbols for them. When demonstrating to a group of Key Stage 2 children, I made a single black dot to show that I felt lonely as a child when my grandmother died. I then immediately balanced this by printing a black dot among a group of dots to symbolise my family around me. I found this encouraged the children to express their feelings more deeply through the printing or speak more openly about them.

Show the children how placing the dots evenly and alternating the colours gives a neat and satisfying appearance to the work. An Aborigine would adopt a certain animal, insect or bird as their own personal symbol. When the dot patterns and journeys are completed, children can decorate any empty areas with an animal of their choice using the cotton bud as a tool for painting as well as for printing.

Figure 5 This illustration is a composite of images taken from children's work and Aboriginal art, intended to show a range of ideas. The dots and shapes outlined in thin pen represent areas where white paint was used.

Further ideas (Reception–Year 6)

Costume   Try Aboriginal printing on cloth instead of paper. Dye white cotton T-shirts in plant dyes (see History – Art) before printing designs as described above but using fabric paints. These can then be worn for Aboriginal dance. Masks can also be made, or you can use face paints to decorate the face symbolically.

Dance   Obtain a recording of Australian music such as *Baka* by Outback. As well as journeys, motifs for your dance could include boomerangs, kangaroos and other animals, tracking and hunting.

Literacy

Journals and souvenirs

The saving of memories is a popular and valuable way of recording journeys and remembering destinations. Producing a journal consolidates the work for children and allows them to relive the experience. Various ways are suggested here to suit different age ranges.

Suitable for   Whole class or group, Reception to Year 6 (the type of journal will vary).

You will need   Any or all of the following are very helpful: For Key Stages 1 and 2, photograph albums, diaries and scrapbooks, old or contemporary; books about famous journeys, especially if written by those who undertook them. For Key Stage 1, *Mouse's Scrapbook* by Michelle Cartlidge

(Campbell Books, ISBN 1–85292–241–9, a tiny book with removable souvenirs) and *The Train Ride* by June Crebbin (Walker Books, ISBN 0–7445–4701–6, a rhythmic rhyming story of a journey, also available as a Story Sack with figures, games and puzzles); notebooks in which to keep the journal (older children can design and make their own as part of the project).

Introduction

Talk with the children about special journeys you have made. They may be short or long, local or distant. Discuss the purpose of the journey – was it to buy something specific, to attend an event, to visit somebody, to experience a new place? When journeys are significant people often record them. Discuss ways in which a journey could be recorded – photographs, video, postcards or letters to friends, written diary, scrapbook, published autobiography, box of souvenirs and so on. Look at any examples you have collected.

The literacy activity

Key Stage 2 children can choose a journey they have made themselves or a journey made by someone in a book, real (such as Florence Nightingale's to the Crimea) or imaginary (Harry Potter's first journey to Hogwarts School). Once the purpose has been established they should then decide what form their journal should take in order to meet this purpose. It might be a diary written on a daily basis, with dates printed at the top of each page, or a book with alternate plain and lined pages for photographs, souvenirs and notes, or a journal divided into categories such as booking information, intended itinerary, maps, diary section and a folder at the back for keepsakes.

When the book has been designed and made, children need to think about the intended readers. Is it to be a book to share memories with others, or a private diary? This decision will determine the style of writing to be used in the book. Souvenirs can be real objects collected from an actual journey, or they can be made by the child, e.g. the nurse's band worn by Florence Nightingale at Scutari, a handmade train ticket to Hogwarts, etc.

Key Stage 1 children can make a small book of souvenirs of a journey similar to *Mouse's Scrapbook*, with each page containing a handmade souvenir (ticket, menu, photo, etc.) in a simple pocket (rectangle of paper glued around three edges and attached to the page) and a small amount of explanatory writing. *The Train Ride* by June Crebbin (see above) is a useful book for this, as all children can make a book about the journey described in it. I found it helpful to act out the journey with the children as a simple drama, sitting on the train and getting off to visit each of the sites mentioned in the book. From each site we collected a souvenir (imaginary in the drama, but made by the children later for their journals) – some wool from the sheep, a photograph of the horse, a piece of straw from the farm, a biscuit wrapper from lunchtime, a feather from the goose, some grains of sand from the beach, and so on. (Bear in mind that all souvenirs need to be flat if they are to be stuck into a book!) You can, of course, make up your own drama journey, on a train or otherwise (see Journeys – Drama.)

Further ideas (Reception–Year 6)

Ants' Journeys   An environmental close observation game for outside. Children should work in pairs on a natural surface such as grass or woodland floor. The two children kneel facing each other with a maximum of 30 cm between them (see Figure 6 overleaf). Each imagines that he/she is an ant journeying to meet the other ant halfway across the space. Child 1 looks hard at the ground immediately in front of him and describes to child 2 the difficulties of his journey, observing every detail in turn: 'I'm just climbing over a piece of broken leaf – the edge is quite sharp – oh! I've slipped'. Child 2 describes the journey from her end: 'The blades of grass are so tall I'm going to climb one to look ahead . . . ugh! A raindrop has slid down the blade and drenched me.' They continue until they meet.

Figure 6 Ants' journeys

Mapwork   Help children to make a map of a journey. This could be a class or group project, or done individually. Look at large and small scale maps first. Older children should aim for as accurate a map as possible and include ordnance survey symbols. Younger children can be helped to draw a bird's eye view of their journey, learning how to put significant points in sequence and how things such as buildings and fields will look from above. Small maps could be included in the journals. Children can also draw a map of the ants' journeys described above.

Choose a starting point and a destination on a map. Ask the children to describe as accurately as possible in speech or writing how to get to one point from the other.

For further map-based work see Feelings –Drama, and for related work on journeys using travel brochures, see Rainforest – Drama.

Chapter 5

Rainforest

The rainforest is rightly a popular topic in schools as it offers a wealth of opportunity for children to learn about plants, animals, ecology, sustainability, materials, conservation, world resources, injustice and people in other lands. But it can also open children's minds to beauty and wonder, and the emotions associated with these. Both the practical and the aesthetic are explored in the ideas below.

Drama

A travel brochure drama

Travel brochures are a wonderful free drama resource for teachers. They provide factual details and visual images sufficient to stimulate children's imagination and to plan a trip, which can be simple or realistically detailed as is appropriate for the children's age and understanding.

Suitable for   Whole class, Reception–Year 6. The drama below is geared to Key Stage 2, but is easily simplified for younger children.

You will need   A current travel brochure (freely available from travel agents) for the area you wish to visit. Look for a brochure with plenty of photographs, facts and descriptions, offering tours which lend themselves to educational experience (e.g. staying in a group shelter in the forest rather than in hotels!) The GAP (Great Adventure People) brochure is packed with information of this kind. See *Further ideas*, below, for useful websites.

Optional, but enormously evocative, are recordings of the sounds of the rainforest, available from New Age mail order companies and ethnic shops. An example is *Amazonian Atmospheres*, Pierre Huguet, Sittelle Publications, ref. 34510.

Introduction

This is another example of a drama which can either be used to launch a topic (in this case the rainforest) and engage the children's interest so that they are eager to learn more, or to culminate a topic so that the knowledge they have built up can be used within it. In either case you need to be very clear about your aims for the drama so that it does not simply become 'pretending to be on holiday', and to equip yourself with enough information to meet these aims (just as you would if you were doing a straightforward 'chalk and talk' lesson). You might, for example, want children to appreciate the diversity of wildlife in the rainforest, in which case you need to know a range of creatures' names and habits. Or you might want them to learn about the dangers of the rainforest and survival techniques, or how the forest is being spoiled, or the importance of teamwork and obeying instructions when on a guided trek.

Select the parts of the brochure you want to use. I find it helpful to put up on the wall any photos from the brochure which show aspects of the tour, so that all children can see them. When working with younger children, you can show them the brochure and explain that we are going on one of the tours in it. Older children can be given copies of the relevant pages to study before the drama commences.

When introducing the drama to the children, be realistic – you cannot undertake an 18-day tour in a drama lesson! Choose one part of the tour to focus on, say the day you first enter the Amazon rainforest. As suitable preparation for the drama, especially with Key Stage 2, talk to the children about what has gone before, and how they would be feeling by this stage of the tour (in the brochure I used, it was day 12). Friendships would have been forged, and a closeness built up based on unique experiences shared. You might be physically tired, yet anxious not to miss anything; looking forward to going home, yet not wanting to leave.

The drama

When the children are prepared for the drama, stand up and introduce yourself as the guide for this part of the tour. Make clear the position so that the children understand their role. You can always have a clipboard or notebook with the information you need. For example, you might say: 'Well, I hope you feel relaxed after our short flight from Cuzco, because we're in for some energetic walking later today! We've now arrived in Puerto Maldonado, in the lowlands of the Amazon rainforest. Soon we'll board a motorised canoe and travel to the Tambopata Forest Reserve. I would ask you, please, ladies and gentlemen, to keep as quiet as possible on this journey, not only out of respect for the wildlife, but also so that you can fully appreciate the sounds of the forest. Do look out for macaw, parrots and river otters among other species.'

You can then usher the children into the canoe, seating them in rows to give the impression of a long, narrow boat. The photographs in the brochure shown to them previously will have equipped them with a visual image. You can now play a recording of the sounds of the rainforest, which will help you to point out 'sightings' as you travel along.

On arrival at the reserve equip children with additional facts to strengthen their experience. 'The reserve holds the world record for the most bird sightings in any one area.' (You can carry with you a book of Amazonian birds so that you can look up what you 'spot'.) 'As you move further into the rainforest you will notice a change in the air – it becomes moister and quite heavily perfumed with the blossoms of some of the trees.' 'You'll notice an increase in the number of butterflies, some of them huge, which feed on the nectar.'

Children will probably want to ask questions, not all of which you may be able to answer. Do not let this worry you – instead, have a notebook with you and stay in role as you jot down their questions. 'I'm not certain of the answer to that, but back at camp I'll look it up for you.' Such questions can then be used as follow-up research to the drama. Conversely some children will have knowledge which they can offer to the drama, from their own reading, hearsay or experience. Encourage them to use their knowledge in the drama. If a child is particularly knowledgeable about an area relevant to the drama, they may be able to take a role as an additional guide. (See *Further ideas*, below.)

The drama can then incorporate the experiences you have chosen to include, such as climbing a canopy tower or rope bridge to get a bird's eye view of the Amazon, learning about the uses of medicinal plants, or visiting the Tambopata Research Center, famous for its macaw clay lick and monkey population. A suitable ending might be hiking to the night's camp, removing rucksacks and talking quietly about the day's experiences while the Amazon rainforest recording is played again.

Further ideas (Key Stage 2)

Children as guides   The children can carry out their own research into a specific area, such as how monkeys live in colonies, or where humming birds live and what they eat. Rather than recording this as a piece of written work or a presentation to the class, use the children as guides in the drama: 'At this point in our journey I'd like to hand you over to Laura's group, who are experts on this particular type of tree.' This gives weight to children's expertise and a chance for them to show their knowledge.

Camping diary   Ask the children to follow the drama with the diary entry they might have made in camp that night, or a letter home about the day's experiences. Alternatively you might make a video diary.

Websites

<www.GAPAdventures.com> has information on projects supporting communities in Latin America, including the unique Rio Muchacho Environmental School, traditional textiles and Ecopaper.

<www.conservation.org> Conservation International works to improve ecosystems without depleting natural resources.

<www.ecotourism.org> and <www.toinitiative.org> Developing tourist opportunities that benefit local cultures and wild areas.

Dance

Preparing for a celebration

A very adaptable dance/drama based on a traditional rainforest community, for all ages. You can use any suitable music, and the suggested ideas can be mixed with or replaced by some of your own.

Suitable for   Whole class, Reception-Year 6. For young children the dance below can be simplified and shortened. With older children, work on higher levels of precision and sensitivity in the way they portray the ideas.

You will need   Choreographed music: *Earth Healer* by Medwyn Goodall, side A (New World Cassettes 218). Suggested alternative music: Any suitably soothing/rhythmic rainforest music, such as pan pipes. Try New Age or ethnic shops. Photographs of people who live in the rainforest (sometimes on travel brochures) are useful to give children clear visual images for the dance, or you may be able to obtain a video.

Introduction

Look at any photographs or books you have which show traditional rainforest communities. Discuss the differences between their lives and ours. What knowledge and understanding do these people have which we do not? What can we learn from them? Compare the things we consider important with the things which are important to them.

Compile a list of activities which might be incorporated into the dance. The suggestions below begin with everyday activities and lead to preparations for a festival, but you can choose, or add, your own. Whatever the activities, it is important that they are enacted as accurately and seriously as possible. Aim for a feeling of respect for the people being portrayed.

To achieve this, I find the drama technique known as 'the mantle of the expert' useful. This simply means that clothing someone in a mantle and telling him he is a king can bring about a belief in him that this is so. (Conversely, as many will know from experience, label a child as a poor singer or writer and he will believe it, often for life.) In this case, tell the children that they are people who have lived in the rainforest all their lives. Let them decide who they are. They can be a man, woman or child.

Important tip   When taking on such roles in drama or dance, explain that children can be only *their own age or above*. If this is not made clear you will have large numbers of babies and toddlers – not useful in drama! They should get into family groups of three, four or five. Both sexes should be represented in each family, either in reality or by taking on opposite roles (though in practice, I find that while girls are sometimes willing to be a grandfather or father, it does not always work the other way around!)

Give the children some time to decide on who is who in their family group, so that if you asked them to introduce each other, they could do so. For example, a group might be made up of a father, mother, grandmother, uncle and son.

Now tell the children that it is an ordinary morning in the rainforest. You are completely used to being here – you know every sound, scent, plant and creature. You know all the people in your community. What are you busy doing? You can choose any activity – making a blowpipe, tool or musical instrument, cleaning an animal skin, weaving a garment, making a shelter, pounding grain, etc. Whatever you are doing, you have done it a thousand times before, and you are an expert at it. It is ordinary to you, but you are giving it your full concentration.

When given this information about themselves children will often mime more accurately and show greater absorption in the task than otherwise. Work at making the movements convincing. If you are throwing a weapon, are you conveying its shape and weight in the way you hold it? Are you tracking the prey silently and fixing your eyes on the target first?

After a while ask children to incorporate other members of the community into their actions. Perhaps you have caught a bird and want to take it to someone you know will pluck and cook it. In return, the cook may ask for a new knife, which you will need to make. Work on building up relationships within the community, without the use of speech.

The dance

0.00   The scene opens with children working individually in a space at their chosen task, giving it full concentration. Encourage a range of shapes – sitting, kneeling, squatting, stooping, standing – to create a balance. Gradually, a few at a time, the children can cross over to other children showing them what they have done, sharing tasks or asking for help.

0.32   At the change in the music, children move into their family groups, each sitting in a small circle. They carefully sew or make the special clothing for the festival, stringing leaves to make waistbands or head-dresses, threading beads for necklaces and bracelets.

0.53   The guitar entry is the signal for the preparations to begin. All movements should be smooth – discourage rushing from task to task, encourage one unhurried pace throughout the workspace. The families rise and first prepare themselves, stepping into the river or under a waterfall, washing faces and bodies. In pairs they groom each other's hair with respect and care. Each person dresses, helping each other place the head-dresses, waistbands and jewellery which have special meaning for them.

1.56   At the quiet change in the music, children move into pairs. Sitting, standing or kneeling, they use a finger to stir a mixture (perhaps of mud or plant material) in the palm of their hand and apply patterns to the face and body of their partner. Children can look at photographs and copy actual patterns or make up their own meanings – a wiggly line on each cheek or arm to represent the river or a snake, a circle on the forehead for the sun, etc. When this is done seriously and sensitively it can form a mesmerising and moving interlude in the dance.

2.29   The beats resume in the music and the children work individually at the tasks involved in preparing food – hunting, skinning, cleaning, cutting, cooking. After working

Figure 7 Rainforest dance at **1.56**

individually, children can begin to cross the space to relate to others, then cross in twos to make up groups of four, so that movement and interest is maintained and an increasingly busy atmosphere is built up.

3.54 At the big key change, each person lifts the dish they have prepared and places it carefully in the middle of the workspace. Depending on the nature of your celebration you may want to perform some ritual, such as raising each dish before presenting it. Children stand around the food, forming a square. When all are in place everyone sits down. The four children at the corners of the square rise, and each lifts a dish from the centre and serves clockwise along one side of the square, sitting at the end of the line. Everyone eats the food (again, encourage accurate miming rather than a repeated raising of the hand to the mouth – what are you holding? How do you bite it? How long does it take to chew?) and the four children at the corners again rise, lift a dish and serve clockwise along one side of the square. Everyone eats again. This pattern is repeated until each of the four children has served each side of the square. This gives a feeling of shared ritual reserved for a special occasion such as a festival.

4.58 At the singing chords, the meal ends and the children rise and step back slightly so that the square becomes a circle. You will need to decide what it is you are celebrating, and one leader should be chosen to instigate movements suitable for your celebration. For example, a celebration of the plants in the rainforest could begin with slowly kneeling, making a small hole in the earth with a finger, holding up a seed to the sky, planting it in the hole, smoothing the soil, raising both hands and flickering the fingers down to the ground to represent rain, and finally bringing the hands together in the shape of a shoot, slowly standing up, raising the hands above the head and spreading them out to represent the plant opening its leaves. All the movements should be smooth and slow enough to ensure that every child has time to copy the leader exactly so that everyone's movements are synchronised.

With the right leader, this is a very effective way of creating a strong visual pattern in dance.

5.25   Fade the music down very gradually. Children turn outwards from the circle and slowly walk away.

Further ideas (Reception–Year 6)

Whole school involvement   In one school, I worked with each of the four classes to produce a series of dances to tell the story of a rainforest. Years 2 and 3 began with a dance showing the birth of the forest, the first seeds sprouting to a recording of drips of water, and then gradually growing into a wide range of strange plants, creepers and lianas as the music built up. Reception to Year 1 showed the contrasting animals of the forest such as sloth, monkey, tree frog, crocodile and snake, concentrating on their different ways of moving. Years 4–5 performed the dance described above, while Year 6 built a powerful dance showing man's destruction of the rainforest, using all their bodies to create one cutting, sweeping, slashing machine which moved forwards relentlessly. To poignant music the trees gradually fell and disintegrated. As they lay still the recording of the drips of rain was played again, and a child from Reception picked her way through to the middle and planted a single seed, so that the dance finished with a note of hope.

Rainforest listening game   A good introductory or cooling-down activity for use in a dance lesson. See *Further ideas* following Rainforest – Literacy, p. 41.

Art

3-D magazine collages

An approach to collage which gives unusual and sometimes rather surreal results. The rainforest is an excellent topic for this technique.

Suitable for   Whole class or groups. The best results are achieved with Years 3–6, though able Year 2s can also respond well if the concept is clearly explained to them.

You will need   A collection of magazines, particularly gardening and cookery based, containing colour photographs (a minimum of one magazine per two children is recommended); background paper (A3 maximum); scissors; twist-up glue sticks. Books and photographs of jungle and rainforest trees, flowers and animals are useful for inspiration, as are the jungle paintings of Henri Rousseau.

Introduction

If the children are not already familiar with the lush richness of the rainforest, its colours, fruits, birds and leaves, spend some time looking at photographs and paintings of these. Then show the children a gardening magazine. Can they see anything in it that reminds them of the rainforest? Children might point to a page showing glossy green leaves or exotic blossoms. Now show them a cookery magazine. Is there anything here that reminds them of the rainforest? Begin to point things out to them – 'these slices of red pepper look like a parrot's tail. If I cut out this lemon slice and stuck this black olive in the centre of it, what a wonderful toucan's eye it would make.'

Show the children another magazine and teach them to turn it upside down before leafing through it. This lessens the tendency to read it or to interpret the pictures in the normal way.

Viewed from a different angle, the pictures reveal new possibilities to the eye. A woman's long hair from an advertisement could become a twisted plant dangling from a tree. The shining side of a car might be perfect for the skin of a tree frog.

The art activity

Begin by asking children to cover the whole of their paper with a suitable background. Double-page spreads of gardens from gardening magazines are ideal for this, but you can use any green scraps from the pages. The best technique is to flick through one or two upside-down magazines and tear out anything suitable, putting it in a pile as you go along. When the pile is big enough, select from it and stick the pieces down – there is no need to neaten them with scissors for the background. Any unsuitable portions, such as writing, a garden bench or gate, can be covered later, but it is important to have no plain paper showing, and covering the whole background gives a depth and richness to the finished collage.

Now flick through other magazines, tearing out as you go anything which might come in useful for a tree trunk, leaf, flower, fruit, bird's bill, etc. Do not be too selective at this stage – anything you reject later might well be useful to someone else. When you have a good collection, look carefully at how the pieces could be used. You do not have to make complete creatures – you could make, say, part of a snake from a gold necklace and cover up the missing part with leaves. To give added interest, animals can be partially attached rather than glued down flat to give a 3-dimensional quality – an exotic butterfly can have its wings and antennae raised from the surface, or a snake can be looped up.

When features such as animals and birds are in place, complete the collage by adding foliage to cover any missing parts (as in the snake) or unwanted writing, etc. These can also be attached in a similar way. Try glueing a leaf only by its top end, or fold it down the middle and stick down the two outer edges so that the middle fold is raised.

Further ideas

Things are not what they seem   Challenge children to find work by artists who used one thing to represent another. Picasso's sculptures using items such as a bicycle seat for the head of a bull; *The Gardener* by Guiseppe Arcimboldo (1527–1593), a face made up of garden produce; and Tessa Traeger's computerised image of Monet's bridge made entirely of vegetables, are examples.

Seascapes   Magazine collage also lends itself well to underwater scenes. Beautiful pebbles can be cut to form sea beds, tropical fish created from dishes in food features, and salads make convincing seaweed!

Weave an emotion   Years 5 and 6 can try creating thought-provoking artwork from two magazine photographs. Search for pictures which seem to link or contrast in some way. Cut one into horizontal strips and one into vertical and weave them together so that parts of each are visible. Examples might be a photograph of lush rainforest and a raging fire, perhaps entitled 'Destruction' or 'Thoughtlessness'; a top of the range car and an eye depicting 'Envy'; or a very old and a very young face for 'Nostalgia'.

Literacy

Preposition poems (Years 3–6)

A simple formula to help children compose lines of poetry while still allowing the imagination free reign.

Suitable for   Whole class, groups, pairs or individuals, Years 3–6.

You will need   Stimulus in the form of books, pictures or previous work on the rainforest; whiteboard for shared ideas; pencils and paper.

Introduction

A preposition is a word used before a noun or pronoun to indicate its relationship to that word, as in '*under the chair*', '*on the shelf*'. I find the following way of teaching children the concept is enjoyable and helps them remember it easily.

I hold in my hand a small object, such as a button or a piece of chalk, which I show to the children.

'I'm going to put this chalk in different places, and then say a sentence about it. In the sentence I shall miss a word out, and you have to tell me what the missing word is. You'll know where the missing word goes because I shall make a little sound like this.' (I make a short sound such as '*mm*'.) 'Let's have a practice.' I hold the chalk over the top of my head, just above my hair. 'The chalk is *mm* my head. What's the missing word?' The children may think of '**above**', '**over**', '**near**' or '**outside**', but they may not have '**on top of**' or '**higher than**' as these are more than one word. As you gather correct suggestions write them on the whiteboard.

Continue holding the chalk in different positions, saying the same sentence ('the chalk is *mm* my head') each time, and writing the prepositions on the board:

> to the side of your head – *near, beside, by, alongside, outside*
> under your chin – *under, below, underneath, beneath, near, by, outside*
> resting on top of your head – *on, upon*
> touching your cheek – *against*
> at the back of your head – *behind, near, by, outside*
> and finally hold it (carefully!) in your mouth – *in, inside, within*

There are, of course, other prepositions, such as *across, among, at, between, towards*, but the above list is suitable to start work on the poem. When you have your list on the board you can explain that these words are all called *prepositions* – easy to remember, because they each tell us the *position* of something.

The literacy activity

For me, composing the first poem as a class effort is the most helpful way to get children launched on this activity, after which they often want to compose further poems individually or in pairs.

Begin by choosing a noun together, in this case *rainforest*. Then select three of the prepositions from the board to begin the three lines of your poem. (Later, children may wish to write more lines, but three is a good number to begin with.) The following is the development of a lesson with a Year 3–4 class who had been studying the rainforest.

After discussing which three prepositions would give the best overall picture of the rainforest, the class chose *above*, *beneath* and *inside*. I explained that the first line of the poem would therefore begin 'Above the rainforest . . .'.

What *is* above the rainforest? What picture do we want to give in our poem? If someone had never heard of the rainforest, how could we put over to them what this part of it is like?

The children's first ideas included such phrases as 'there are birds flying to and fro' or 'the sky is bright blue'. I said that this could be describing the school playground. *What* are the birds like, and *how* do they fly? Is the sky the same as where we live, or might it be different? The children began to suggest adjectives for the birds and the sky – 'screeching', 'squawking', 'tropical', 'blazing'. We listed these on the board and tested them aloud for sound, rhythm and atmosphere.

I asked them which were the most boring or ordinary words in their sentences. They decided on 'and', 'there are', and 'is'. We looked at ways of trying to replace these. After working on the first line until we were satisfied, we did the same with the second and third. In the time available, the final version read:

Above the rainforest screeching birds swoop in the colourful sky.
Beneath the rainforest strange insects scutter in the deep dark earth.
Inside the rainforest endangered species stalk and creep.

The poem was later used for choral narration, accompanied by percussion instruments, to open a dance piece showing the life and death of the rainforest.

Further ideas (Years 3–6)

Riddles   A variation on the preposition poem. Take the question 'Where am I?' Each line of your poem should be a clue beginning with a preposition. For example:

Around me wave stalks of gold.
Beneath me harvest mice forage . . . (a cornfield)

or

Below me, gloopy gunge gurgles.
Before me, monstrous knees steam . . . (a bath overflow)

Using other nouns   The preposition formula can be applied to many other subjects, such as:

Above the ice . . . (rosy-cheeked skaters dart and shout)
Below the ice . . . (fish lurk in the silent depths)
Inside the ice . . . (trapped bubbles glitter like frozen diamonds)

Other poetry formulae   See Materials – Literacy for similar starting points for poetry writing.

Rainforest listening game   All the children stand with you in a circle. There is only one rule – each person must only look at and copy the person to their left. You, the teacher, hold out your left palm in front of you and gently rub two fingers of your right hand to and fro on it, which makes a slight sound. The child to your right should copy this and it should then gradually pass around the circle. When it is about two thirds round, you begin to gently patter your two fingers on your palm instead. This gradually passes round. Continue as follows:

tapping harder with two fingers at the same time
clapping fairly gently
clapping hard
slapping thighs quickly and alternately
clapping hard
clapping fairly gently
tapping with two fingers on palm
rubbing two fingers on palm
stopping all movement (this too should pass around the circle gradually)

At first the temptation is for all children to look at and copy the teacher. The game should be practised on different occasions until it is smoothly carried out. The result is a remarkable sound effect of a tropical storm in a rainforest, useful both as a warming-up and a cooling down activity for a variety of lessons. See also *Further ideas*, *4-part orchestra*, following Machines – Dance.

Chapter 6

Seasons

Recognising the pattern of the seasons is a fundamental part of our understanding of the world. The seasons of the year have a bearing on almost every aspect of our lives, involving all five of our senses and offering a wealth of material to explore, making them a frequent topic for study in schools.

Drama

'The Land of Banned Birthdays'

In this drama, which can be extended to more than one session, children are given the opportunity to 'visit' each season and experience the qualities that define it. The birthday theme gives children a sense of ownership of 'their' season – the one in which they were born.

Suitable for   Whole class, Reception, Years 1 and 2.

You will need   A list of the months of the year, with the names of the children born in that month written beside each one.

Introduction

Tell the children that they are going to visit a land which is very sad. The king there is old, grumpy and miserable. He hates to see people enjoying themselves, but what he hates most of all is to see people having birthday parties. No one ever gives him presents or birthday cakes, and so he can't stand seeing children being given them. He usually just moans and groans about it, but yesterday a boy had a birthday party in his house, which is opposite the palace, and the king saw it all through the window. He was so jealous that he announced that he will ban all birthdays for ever. No one will be allowed to mention their birthdays, sing 'Happy Birthday' or send cards – unless someone is brave enough to visit the Lords of the Seasons at the far corners of the earth and complete a task for each of them. The king chose this purposely because he knows no one will be able to do it. It's a long, long journey, and the weather can be terrible . . .

The drama

Hopefully the children will volunteer to go on the expedition! Ask them what they think they should pack. They will be visiting the freshest spring, the hottest summer, the windiest, wettest autumn and the iciest, snowiest winter. Pack your suitcase – umbrellas, suntan lotion, bikinis, wellingtons, fleeces, mittens, sunglasses, etc. Off we go. Has everyone got their season ticket?

  You may want to devote some time here to devising your method of transport, a vehicle which can cope with every kind of temperature and weather condition. This can form a whole session in itself, and may involve designing and drawing the vehicle on paper and building it in the drama. You can then climb into the vehicle and journey to your first destination.

You arrive in the land of spring. Feel the air, take a look around, and put on appropriate clothing. What can you see, hear, touch and smell? Walk about, reacting to the freshness, the blossoming trees, the sky, the birdsong. Roll on the grass. Smell the flowers.

You, the teacher, can now step into the role of the Lord (or Lady, Queen, King, as you wish) of Spring. Describe your clothing – a long, green gown made of daffodil leaves, birds in your hair and two snowdrops for earrings. Tell the children their task – spring is a time for spring cleaning. They must spring clean everything that they see. Vacuum the grass, polish the trees, dust the flowers, wipe the birds. Keep going round, inspecting their work and noting any imperfections. When you are satisfied, ask which children have their birthday in spring (March, April, May). As a special treat, these children can pick any flowers they like to take home. They give them to the other children who can tie them into beautiful bouquets.

Off you go in the vehicle again, making any adaptations necessary to travel into the heat of summer. It's so hot when you arrive that you need to put on your sunbathing gear. This time the Lord of Summer wears a dazzling suit of sunshine, designer sunglasses and a head-dress of vivid summer flowers. The children's task is to get the land ready for the summer tourists. They must iron the sand, mow the cliff tops and tidy the seagulls' nests. (You can, of course, add any other tasks that are appropriate.) The summer birthday children (June, July, August) can each build a sandcastle as their treat. Others can visit the sandcastles and photograph the birthday children beside them.

The vehicle then takes you to the land of autumn. You can hear the wind whistling as you approach. Look out of the vehicle windows and change into the right clothing. The leaves whirl around you and it's raining. The Lord of Autumn wears a cloak of rustling russet leaves, a necklace of fruits, acorns and nuts and a crown of chrysanthemums. The task is to sweep up every leaf to be seen into a huge pile, whilst battling with the weather. The birthday children (September, October, November) can then jump in the leaves for a special treat, while the others count their jumps (one for each month of the year).

Finally you visit the coldest place – the land of winter. Dress as warmly as you can! The Lord of Winter wears a sparkling, frosty suit studded with tinkling icicles, a scarf of snowflakes and a white fur circlet. The task is to build him the hugest snow palace ever seen. It must be beautiful, safe and strong. When it is complete the winter birthday children (December, January, February) can put on an ice-skating show for the other children to watch and applaud (or, if you are feeling up to it, have a snowball fight.)

Shivering, you return to the Land of Banned Birthdays. Gather the class together and decide how to end the session. Did the king allow birthdays from then on? How could we help him not to feel jealous and grumpy? Why do you think he has no friends? What about having a birthday party for everyone in the land, and inviting the king to it?

You can end the session with an imaginary party with presents, games, singing 'Happy Birthday' and a huge cake with candles for everyone to blow out, or this could form a further session, with children planning games, baking and organising the event. The role of the king could be played by yourself or a child, and he could be questioned about how he feels.

Further ideas (Reception, Years 1–2)

Collage lords   The costumes visualised in the drama make good subject matter for collages. Collages for each of the four lords could be made by the children whose birthdays fall in the appropriate season.

Tourist brochures   Ask the children to write promotional material to attract tourists to visit the lands of spring, summer, autumn and winter.

Suitcases   Make a collection of pictures, objects and clothing appropriate to the four seasons and ask children to sort them into four suitcases ready to go on the journey. The suitcases can also act as dressing up boxes.

Diaries   Ask each child to draw the treat they were given for doing the task (picking flowers, building sandcastles, jumping in leaves, ice-skating) and write a sentence about it.

Dance

Spring in the garden

A gentle dance depicting aspects of the garden in spring – planting, growing and garden features.

Suitable for   Whole class, Years 1–4. Easily manageable by older children but content is more suitable for the younger age range.

You will need   Choreographed music: Gabriel Fauré's 'Le Jardin de Dolly' from his *Dolly Suite*. This should be easy to obtain, and the other five pieces which make up the suite were also written with a child in mind. Suggested alternative music: the atmosphere should be gentle, pastoral and simple. An orchestral version of *An English Country Garden* would be suitable, as would parts of Delius's *On Hearing the First Cuckoo in Spring*, Beethoven's *Pastoral Symphony* or Vaughan Williams' *The Lark Ascending*.

Introduction

The timings given below will vary depending on which recording you use (mine is the 1982 version by the Academy of St Martin in the Fields conducted by Neville Marriner) but the piece is made up of clear phrases which will assist in learning the dance. Explain to the children that the dance shows the story of what happens in a garden in spring. Plants grow from seeds and bulbs, trees break out in leaf, people begin to enjoy playing, working and sitting in their gardens, digging, putting in new plants and building arbours, seats and pergolas. Finally, as spring fully develops, the flowers and trees blossom.

Before beginning the dance, divide the children into four groups.

The dance

Position the children in their groups, one group in each corner of the workspace. Each group forms a small circle, and each child makes a small, tight and low shape to represent a seed or bulb. Encourage variation in the shapes for different plants.

0.00   The piece begins with four short flute phrases of six beats each. On the first phrase, the children in Group 1 grow, rising, twisting and swaying their arms to resemble young plants. They should aim to end up in varying shapes, some kneeling, some standing, some tall, some spread out, some touching or tangling with others to make a pleasing final shape in their circle. Encourage interesting shapes made with the legs but emphasise that children must be able to hold their final position comfortably for a while.

Group 2 grows in a similar way on the second phrase, followed by Groups 3 and 4 on the third and fourth phrases. Each group holds their position still while other groups grow.

0.23   All groups imagine a slight breeze in the garden and sway gently for six beats, moving arms, upper bodies and fingertips. The next six beats are used for the whole class to form a circle of arches. Each child should move to join a partner who is suitably near them. One child in each pair faces into the circle and one out. They join palms above their heads to form a pointed arch. Work at making this circle of arches as even as possible and practise getting into exactly the same place each time.

0.34   If there is an odd number of children in the class, the child without a partner (you can choose who this should be as it is a key role!) can run gently through the arches for the next twelve beats. If there is an even number of children, two can run through, keeping opposite each other in the circle.

0.46   The circle breaks up and children find an individual space, evenly spread out. They work alone for 24 beats on their imaginary garden, digging with spade or trowel, sowing seeds, putting in plants, pruning, raking and watering. Practise these tasks, encouraging children to look as absorbed as possible. After a while they can begin to relate to someone near them, sharing tasks and working together.

1.11   When the violins repeat the phrase, the children move (smoothly and without rushing) into groups of two, three or four, again evenly positioned around the workspace. Each group grows slowly into a garden feature – a seat (on which perhaps a child could sit), an arbour, bridge, pergola or shelter. Try to make each structure different. Hold the positions until the end of the phrase. (24 beats in all.)

1.34   The music now moves into a minor key and again four phrases are played. On the first (6 beats) the children from Group 1 return to their original corner and resume their low starting positions. All other children remain in their 'pergola' shapes. On the second phrase Group 2 return and so on with all four groups (warning – Group 4's phrase is shorter than the others – only 3 beats!)

1.56   Four flute phrases again. Repeat instructions for 0.00.

2.19   Two short identical phrases of six beats each. On the first, the two diagonally opposite groups kneel facing inwards, heads down, in a tight circle and remain still. On the second phrase the two remaining groups do likewise. Hold for a further 3 beats.

2.37   On the final chord all children unhurriedly raise their heads and arms and hold the blossom shapes to end the dance.

Figure 8 Spring dance at **2.37**

Further ideas (Reception–Year 6)

Plant dyes   See History – Art for using natural dyes with children.

Miniature gardens   Can be made, with varying degrees of sophistication, by children of any age. For full practical details see the author's *Creative History Activity Packs – Victorians* (see Suggested Further Reading).

Spring greens   Give children small blobs of red, blue, yellow, black and white paints and challenge them to discover how many different greens they can mix with them. Each of the colours must be used, and only greens must be made. Begin by trying a tiny touch of black and quite a lot of yellow. Add more black gradually to darken. Then try the same with blue and yellow. Add red to give browny greens, white to give soft sage greens. Each time they discover a new green, they should paint a differently shaped leaf. For inspiration, show children strips of paint sample cards in the greens range (from DIY stores) and the jungle paintings of Henri Rousseau, particularly *Tropical Storm with Tiger*, which has a huge range of greens and imaginary foliage shapes.

Art

Winter webs

Delicate, moveable sculptures which can be used to create a striking interactive display.

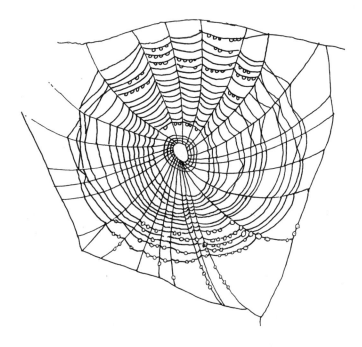

Figure 9

Suitable for   Whole class, individuals, pairs or groups, Years 2–6, though I have also done this with able Year 1s. Younger children (and some older ones) will need help with wire and knotting threads.

You will need   One or more photographs of a spider's web studded with raindrops (or take the children to see a real example if at all possible!) other photographs of raindrops, webs, frosted twigs or frost patterns on windows; a collection of twigs (see note below); secateurs and wirecutters for use by adult; thin wire (easily manipulated by children – can be bought at florists); threads (embroidery thickness) in cold, frosty colours (blues, purples, white, grey, metallic, etc.); beads with fairly large holes in similar colours to threads – glass or clear plastic beads are particularly effective; scissors; white and/or silver paints; paintbrushes.

Note: The twigs should be of a suitable length for the project – about 25 cm minimum and 40 cm maximum. They should not be too fragile as they will be handled a lot, but nor should they be extremely thick, as this will detract from the delicacy of the sculptures. Twigs with others branching from them are the most useful, as they form interesting shapes, but straight twigs can be joined with wire.

Introduction

Show the children the photographs, looking at the delicacy of the web and where the spider chooses to spin it, the way the raindrops look like beads hanging on it, and the effect of the frost. Ask which colours could be described as 'cold' and discuss why this could be. Look at the collection of twigs and show how two or three can be placed together and joined with wire to form a 3-dimensional sculpture which is interesting from all angles, and which would provide a good structure in which a spider could spin a web.

The art activity

Begin by constructing the twig sculptures. You may find that some twigs have enough interest already, so that it is not necessary to join them to others, but two or three twigs are usually needed. Show the children how to join the twigs by wrapping wire in and out of them at the point where they touch (a figure of eight wrapping style will hold much better than a 'round and round', but there are no rules – offer the method of joining to the children as a problem to solve). The overall size of the final structure should be between that of a brick and a shoebox, so that it is manageable by the child, and it should offer spaces across which threads can be strung.

Children should now cut a length of their chosen thread. Their nose to their outstretched hand is a good measurement as this is the length that is manageable by the measurer. Help children to knot one end of their thread to a part of the twig sculpture. A simple double knot is fine, and children can often help each other with this. It is tempting to use Sellotape™ with younger children, but this not only looks unattractive but does not work well, often pulling away from the twig and causing more heartache than tying the knots would have done! Once the thread is knotted the child should thread two or three beads on to it. The thread can now cross to another part of the sculpture and be wrapped tightly around another twig. If there is enough length, thread on two or three more beads and cross to another point before knotting in position. Choose another thread and repeat, but do not overfill the sculpture with thread and beads. This is a case of 'less is more' – it is the spaces, the simplicity and the understatement of these sculptures that gives them their charm.

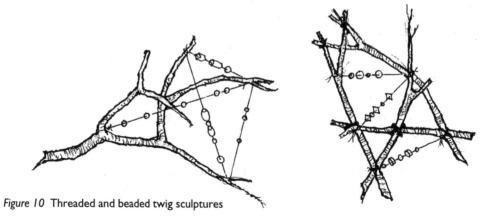

Figure 10 Threaded and beaded twig sculptures

When the sculptures are complete children can touch the twigs with a paintbrush dipped in white or silver paint, frosting them, as nature often does, on one side only. Again, avoid too much painting so that the 'frost' can contrast with the dark twigs.

To display, you can hang the sculptures as mobiles or pin them to display boards with a pinpusher, but they are best placed freely on a plain dark drape so that children can gently lift and tilt them, causing the bead 'raindrops' to run along the threads. The photographs you have used as a stimulus can be displayed on the wall behind them.

Further ideas (Years 1–6)

Seasonal stitchings   Give the children a piece of stockinette (dishcloth) fixed into a small (6–7 cm) circular rubber-edged embroidery frame. Provide as wide a variety of wools as possible and let the children sort these into spring, summer, autumn and winter colours. With a large blunt needle children can make flat or looped stitches (loops can be left, or snipped when complete to resemble grass) to represent plants of each season, aiming to fill the dishcloth as closely as possible (hence the small frame). Older children can sew on beads where appropriate, e.g. brown ovals for autumn acorns, round red beads against dark green wools for winter holly. When complete, remove from frames. Cut circles the same size as the inner frames from stiff card. Stretch stitchings over card circles and glue edges in place on the back. (Do not put any glue on the front of the card or it may seep through the stitching.) Copydex™ is ideal for this as it holds immediately but allows the work to be repositioned if necessary.

Completed leaves   Collect and press autumn leaves, choosing those with several shades. When pressed cut each leaf in two down the central vein. Glue a half leaf slightly to one side of a sheet of white paper, leaving room for the child to paint the other half to match. With a small soft brush, watercolours and careful observation, astonishing matches can be achieved by some children, but this is also good as a colour-mixing exercise for beginners.

Literacy

Seasonal senses

Through reading and writing a poem, children explore the ways in which we sense a season.

Suitable for   Whole class, but also groups, pairs or individuals, Years 2–6.

You will need   Pencils and paper; copies of *The Calendar* by Barbara Euphan Todd (see below).

Introduction

Give the children copies of *The Calendar* by Barbara Euphan Todd and let it be read aloud.

> I knew when Spring was come –
> Not by the murmurous hum
>   Of bees in the willow-trees,
>   Or frills
>   Or daffodils,
> Or the scent of the breeze;
> But because there were whips and tops
> By the jars of lollipops
> In the two little village shops.

I knew when summer breathed –
Not by the flowers that wreathed
   The sedge by the water's edge,
     Or gold
     Of the wold,
Or white and rose of the hedge;
But because, in a wooden box
In the window at Mrs Mock's
There were white-winged shuttlecocks.

I knew when Autumn came –
Not by the crimson flame
   Of leaves that lapped the eaves
     Or mist
     In amethyst
And opal-tinted weaves;
But because there were alley-taws
(Punctual as hips and haws)
On the counter at Mrs Shaw's.

I knew when Winter swirled –
Not by the whitened world,
   Or silver skeins in the lanes
     Or frost
     That embossed
Its patterns on window-panes:
But because there were transfer sheets
By the bottles of spice and sweets
In the shops in two little streets.

The literacy activity

Ask the children questions about the poem, to which they can give verbal or written replies:

1   From the content, how old do you think the writer is? (The interest in the toys and sweets suggests a child; her knowledge of the shops' annual rituals suggests she had witnessed them for several years.)
2   How many shops were there in the village and who kept them?
3   What are alley-taws? (a type of marble for children's games.)
4   What is meant by 'punctual as hips and haws'?
5   How can you tell that the poem is not modern? (The toys mentioned are no longer common; nowadays toys are sold all year round and are not seasonal.)
6   Do you think the writer is being entirely truthful about how she recognises the seasons? (She says she knows them by what is sold in the shops, but also lists all the natural signs of the seasons – which proves that she has noticed them!)
7   Give children five coloured crayons. Ask them to colour any lines, phrases or words in the poem which are to do with the five senses – sight, sound, smell, touch and taste. Use a different colour for each sense.

     Which sense is mentioned most often?
     Which sense is mentioned only once?
     Which sense is not mentioned at all?

8   Is there anything sold in shops today which would tell us what season it was?

Ask children to make four headings – Spring, Summer, Autumn and Winter. Under each one, list the five senses. For each sense, write a phrase or sentence for that sense and that season. For example, for *Autumn – Smell* might be 'bonfire woodsmoke' or 'damp leaves crushed underfoot'. When the choices have been made, use the phrases to build a poem. The poem need not rhyme but it could have a rhythm, as Barbara Euphan Todd's does. It might begin:

> Spring –
> The sight of fresh green shoots.
> The sound of bleating lambs.

Or you could add to it, making another rhythm:

> Spring –
> The sight of fresh green shoots, pushing through earth.
> The sound of bleating lambs, puzzled and new.

Further ideas (Reception–Year 6)

Rules for a season   Years 4–6 could try writing a list of rules for each season to obey, such as 'Spring.

1   Be as confusing as possible – windy one minute, sunny the next, then rain extremely hard.
2   Bulbs in famous places should arrange to be in flower for the tourists on Bank holidays.'

Lists and debate   Children from Reception to Year 6 can make lists of what they like and dislike about a season. Key Stage 2 can use these lists as a basis for a debate, arguing the case for the best season. The class should be divided into eight groups, one for and one against each season. Each group should plan their argument carefully and elect a speaker. The teacher should chair the debate and the rest of the class vote for the best case.

The fifth season   A writing challenge for Years 3–6. If there were a fifth season, what would be its characteristics and what would it be called?

Chapter 7

Machines

Machines have become an integral part of our everyday lives; we are surrounded by them, depend on them, take them for granted and cannot imagine life without them. Their shapes, sounds, designs, movements and functions offer wide opportunities for creative work through history, maths, science, music and design technology as well as the four curriculum areas detailed below.

Drama

'Mr Turner's Will'

All kinds of objects, property and instructions can be left in wills, which makes them an ideal starting point for drama by confronting children with a problem they must solve together. Here, a valuable collection of fairground machinery requires expert care.

Suitable for   Whole class; the wording on the photocopiable sheet is designed for Key Stage 2 but a simpler version can easily be made for Key Stage 1.

You will need   A copy of the will (see photocopiable resource, Figure 11); steam organ recording or similar Victorian-style fairground music; a copy of the Yellow Pages. It is also helpful if children can be shown photographs of fairground rides, preferably from Victorian times.

Introduction

The will given here was designed for a class who had been studying controllable vehicles through Design and Technology and were also involved in a project on the Victorians. You can of course design a will which precisely fits your requirements. Whatever its content, an arresting way to start as you stand up to begin the drama is to produce a letter from the solicitors. You can read this to the class or ask a child to do so. The letter can be very realistic – the one I made bore the address of the school, the sender's address, and yesterday's date, and was written in suitably formal language. If you can find a used, stamped envelope with yesterday's postmark, replace the address with your name and the school's address on a label, and reseal it, so much the better! The letter should say that the solicitors enclose a copy of the will of Josiah Turner, as they understand that your pupils have an unusual degree of expertise in machinery and may be able to fulfil the exact conditions stipulated in its contents. The letter can finish with an invitation to view the rides, which are located in a nearby field. The will can then be read aloud to the children.

The drama

Ask the children for their opinion on this project. Perhaps they are honoured to be approached, or they could be daunted by the task. Look carefully at the details of the will, noting that Mr Turner

This is the last will and testament of me, Josiah Nathaniel Turner, made on the ...... day of .... 20..... in the presence of my solicitors, Jacobson, Roberts and Trent.

As a boy I frequently visited travelling fairgrounds with my father and grandfather, who inspired in me a fascination with fairground machinery. This led to my passion for fairground memorabilia in later life, and over the course of many years I have amassed a large collection of Victorian fairground rides. Having no children, it is my wish that these valuable and beautiful machines should be passed to experts who share my love of the fair. I have appointed my solicitors to seek out after my death a group of people with a knowledge of fairground machinery who will devote time to maintaining these Victorian rides, many of which are steam powered, and allow the public to see them in full use again. Trusting in their choice I leave the following:

One stand of eight swingboats
One merry-go-round
One miniature railway with engine and six carriages
One 'duckpond' with moving ducks as targets for hoop throwing
One 'chairoplane' ride
One Ferris wheel

This will is signed by me   *Josiah N. Turner*

Witnessed by   *R.C. Jacobson*
    P. Roberts
    H. Trent

Figure 11

wants the rides to be enjoyed by the public. Decide on a plan of action, such as dividing the class into six groups so that each group can inspect one machine and report back.

As each group is examining their machine (they can take real notes about its condition if you wish), visit each one to encourage discussion and inject ideas. Some rivets on the swingboats seem to be rusting – can we find someone who will make reproduction Victorian rivets? Has Mr Turner left certificates to show that the machines are in good working order? What fuel will we need for the steam-powered engines and is there a local supplier? (It is good to provide the children with a copy of the Yellow Pages so that they can actually learn what such specialists are called and how to locate them. You can then pretend to telephone them in the drama.)

Each group then reports back to the class, airing its concerns and any problems. The class with whom I worked included the following ideas:

1 Can the miniature train carry adults or only children? If the latter, should we impose an age limit?
2 The duckpond can only be put in motion by inserting an old penny.
3 Some of the authentic Victorian details are no longer safe. For example, the merry-go-round will need to be repainted with lead-free paint.
4 All the machines need thoroughly oiling.

Ask if anyone has a special area of expertise, such as steam-powered engines, pulleys, or cleaning brass pistons, so that they can be called on if necessary. Groups can then start repairing, refurbishing and testing their rides. Encourage the sharing of practical difficulties and using one another's knowledge, using the Yellow Pages and imaginary phones to call for professional advice if needed.

When the fairground is completely safe and ready to open to the public, call another meeting. This time, collect ideas for the grand opening of the fairground. In our case these included:

1 Selling old pennies to the public at the entrance.
2 Offering Victorian refreshments such as home-made lemonade.
3 Dressing in Victorian clothing.
4 Hiring a Victorian barrel organ.
5 Distributing posters around the area detailing the rides.
6 Charging Victorian prices on the first day.
7 Calling the fairground 'The Turner Collection'!

Different groups can be responsible for setting these preparations in motion. The drama ends with the grand opening. Children can take turns running and visiting rides. Aim to recreate a bustling atmosphere, with cries of 'Roll up! Roll up!' and 'Get your pennies here!', etc. This is greatly helped by playing steam organ music or other suitable sound effects.

Further ideas (Key Stage 2)

Character cards   An alternative approach to the fairground theme is to give groups of children character cards (as detailed in Creation – Drama). These could be:

- Gangers (responsible for dismantling/erecting rides at every venue, loading on to trailers, fitting in correct order);
- Administration Staff (dealing with money, answering phone, customer complaints, organising annual venues);
- Drivers (in charge of staff transport, catering vans, caravans, trailers, maintaining all vehicles);
- Caterers (providing all food for staff and customers, planning menus and shifts, health and safety);
- Stallholders (running all stalls, stands and rides);

- Mechanics (responsible for maintenance and safety of all rides and equipment on site);
- Managers (own fairground, employ all staff, liaise with all staff regularly).

Letter   A further approach is to produce a realistic letter from a fictitious company such as 'Whitford's Fairground Enterprises'. Addressed to yourself, it might say:

> It has come to our attention that you will shortly be working with a team of experts on fairground machinery. We understand that these experts, although young, have extensive knowledge and an imaginative and inventive ability.
>
> As one of the top providers of fairground entertainment in the region we are always interested to hear of new ideas for rides, and at the moment particularly so as the region is holding a competition for the most exciting fairground to open the new season.
>
> We would be delighted if your experts could use their inventive powers to bring to life a fairground which would be safe and suitable for all the family.

Children could fulfil the competition brief through drama, dance, art or design technology.

Dance

Clocks and timepieces

Time, by definition, is rhythmical, and all timepieces involve some kind of repetitive movement, so ways of measuring time lend themselves well to being explored through music and dance. This busy, enjoyable dance, showing six different timepieces, needs practice to be neat and precise but offers great opportunities for teamwork.

Suitable for   Whole class, Years 3–6 in the form given, but the ideas could be simplified for Reception–Year 2.

You will need   Choreographed music: *Syncopated Clock* by Leroy Anderson. Suggested alternative music: Kodaly's *Viennese Clock* or any marching, rhythmical piece with a strong beat. A collection of clocks and timepieces (or photographs of them) is very useful as stimulus.

Introduction

Look at the clocks or photographs you have collected. They all share a function, but do they have anything else in common? Look at the ways they move, repetitively and rhythmically, and find ways to imitate these. Make a list of methods of telling the time.

The Year 3 class with whom I first built this dance thought of the following:

sundial	alarm clock
candle	digital clock/watch
water clock	cuckoo clock
sand clock (hour glass)	grandfather clock
dial clock/watch	

Of these, the first three were rejected as not offering enough movement or being too slow for the music. We then explored ways of using the other timepieces in our dance. The class were proudest of their digital clock, which they largely worked out for themselves.

The dance

The children must be in position before the music starts. First, two children represent the hands of a clock. The minute hand lies on her back or stomach, arms above head pointing into the middle of the work space. The hour hand lies on his back or stomach at ninety degrees or more to her, facing inwards, arms tightly by sides, head touching first child's hands. The remaining children sit around them facing inwards in a circle, legs drawn up, heads on knees, to represent a clock face with seconds marked around it.

0.00 All children keep very still during the short tick-tock introduction.

0.05 As the musical theme begins, the minute hand starts to move (in a clockwise direction!) a second at a time by pulling round the circle with her feet. She should not move too fast or she will catch the hour hand up. The hour hand should move almost imperceptibly. The children being the clock face should remain absolutely still and not look up.

0.21 At the repetition of the theme tune, all jump up and quickly move into a predetermined space. This is a chance for children to show their individual ideas, using their bodies to imitate working parts of clocks and watches – cogs, springs, hands, winders – so that the space is filled with rhythmic, swinging, turning and repetitive movements.

0.37 At the key change, twelve children form an hour-glass shape on the floor (see Figure 12) and all remaining children stand inside one end of it to represent the sand. When all are in place the 'sand' starts to walk through and fill the other side. With practice, this can be timed so that at **0.48** (a few jaunty notes on the clarinet) the last child (who should be chosen beforehand for this task) can push through the middle of the hour glass with a cheeky wiggle. (This raised laughter at our performance!)

0.52 The theme is heard again. Children move quickly into pairs to form grandfather clocks, standing one behind the other facing in the same direction. The front child puts his palms together, points his arms downwards and swings them left and right (preferably in time to the music) for the pendulum. The child behind uses her arms to represent the hands of the clock. (Remember these must move clockwise *as seen from the front!*)

1.09 During the 8 second bridge in the music, children divide into four groups, which move to the four corners of the workspace. Each group consists of an alarm clock and several sleepers. The sleepers lie in a row as if in a dormitory asleep. The alarm clock squats near them, head down and still.

1.17 The first alarm bell rings. Group 1's alarm clock does two big jumps to the music, shaking and jangling, arms above head. Group 1 sleepers sit up suddenly, rub eyes, stretch, start dressing, washing, etc. All other dancers in work space remain still.

1.25 Second alarm clock – Group 2 repeats actions above. Group 1 continues waking/getting up.

1.33 Group 3 alarm clock.

1.41 Group 4 alarm clock.

1.47 Short tick-tock. During this it is effective if every child in the room does a yawn and stretch above their heads.

1.51 Theme music returns. Eighteen children form the digital clock face showing 8.59 by lying on the floor (see Figure 13). The dot is formed by a child squatting, head down.

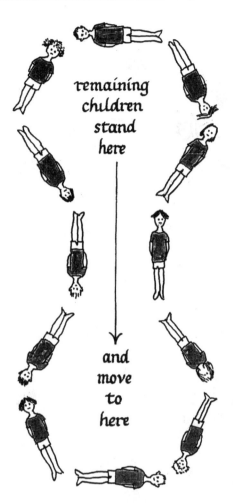

Figure 12 The clock dance at **0.37**

Remaining children in the class line up at the side of the clock as if ready to come in from the playground. In our version, the teacher stood at the front with a whistle in her hand.

2.06 Theme music repeats. Children forming digital clock remain still except for four children (marked A, B, C and D on illustrations) who move quickly to their next position to form **9.00**, (see Figure 14) at which point the line of children is led forward as if into school. (The class chose these times because it was when they came into school in the morning, but you could alter these to suit your particular timetable.)

2.20 All children move quickly into a sitting circle exactly as at the beginning of the dance. Three remain in the middle. Two of these stand opposite each other, arms raised and hands joined into a sloping roof above the third child, who bends down between them.

2.35 After the two beats on the tin drum, the roof opens, the child in the middle jumps up and shouts 'Cuckoo!' and the dance ends.

Figure 13 The clock dance at **1.51**

Figure 14 The clock dance at **2.06**

Further ideas (Key Stage 2)

Poem   A useful resource is the wonderfully evocative poem *The Watch* by May Swenson, suitable for studying with Key Stage 2 children and as a stimulus for writing, music or drawing.

4-part orchestra   A good warm-up for drama, dance or singing, or a music lesson in its own right. Divide the children into four groups and position them around you. Decide on a theme, such as a shop which sells clocks and watches. Take on the role of conductor, bringing in each group at a time with a suitable sound, which can be made with instruments or with the voice. For example, Group 1 could make the sound 'tick tock tick tock tick tock' to establish a rhythm. Bring in Group 2 over them with slow clicking sounds of the tongue. Group 3 could chime 'bing bong' on two notes, and Group 4 call 'cuckoo!' periodically. Introduce signals to indicate louder, softer, stop. Keep the sounds changing to maintain an interesting effect. After a while a child could take on the role of conductor. Other machine themes might be a factory, trains, a fairground or outer space. Or you could try a rainforest, the seaside or a farm.

Art

Painting to music

Machines are rarely silent – one of their most obvious characteristics is sound, usually rhythmical. In the activity below, a piece of music inspired by a machine is in turn used to inspire visual images.

Suitable for   Whole class or group, Reception–Year 6.

You will need   Music: *Short Ride in a Fast Machine* by John Adams, EMI Classics 7243 5 55051 2 5. Other noisy, rhythmic, machine-like music can be used, although *Short Ride . . .* is ideal as it is evocative, exciting and at 4.24 minutes a useful length; large paper; coloured pastels; paints; large and small paintbrushes. Two excellent resources are Georgia O'Keeffe's painting *Blue and Green Music*, and the 7 minute video *Begone Dull Care*, a fascinating and exciting interpretation of jazz music through colours and shapes made in 1949, ideal as an introduction to painting to music for children. It comes accompanied by other short films suitable for children under the title *Animation Classics* (National Film Board of Canada) and can be ordered from Connoisseur Video, 10A Stephen Mews, London W1P 0AX, 0207 957 8957.

Introduction

Show the children the painting by Georgia O'Keeffe. Ask them their views on what inspired the painting. Explain that it was music, and discuss what kind of music it might have been. Sad, slow, loud, jolly? Do you think the artist listened to the music while she was painting the picture?

Now play some of the John Adams piece, asking the children to close their eyes as they listen. Do not tell the children the title of the music at this stage. Fade the music down and ask what they saw while they listened – focus on colours and shapes rather than objects or images. What did the music make them feel and smell? If they were painting to it, how would they move the brush and what marks would they make?

Put a large piece of paper on an easel and have some pastels and paints to hand. Start the music again and demonstrate to the children some of the marks, colours and brush movements you feel like making to it. There are two approaches that can be taken – it is helpful to demonstrate a mixture of the two. Either you can paint *to* the music, making marks actually in time to it (this fills the paper up very quickly) or you can listen with eyes closed for a while, and then paint at leisure the shapes and patterns which you see in your mind, while the music continues to play.

The art activity

Make sure that all children are equipped with everything they need so that getting out of their seats during the music can be avoided. A choice of large and small brushes is a good idea when doing any painting, and is recommended for this work; it makes children take a decision on the kind of marks they want to make. Tell the children how long the piece of music is and ask them to try and keep silent and concentrate for its duration – when the music stops you can take a break and tackle any difficulties. Explain that if they are not happy with what they produce they can alter it as they wish (I try to avoid repeatedly starting the painting all over again except in the event of a major mishap!).

Older children may find it helpful to listen to the piece in its entirety before painting, to help their planning. They may also like to start with scrap paper, making preliminary studies before embarking on a more polished composition.

Switch on the music and be on hand with a cloth for spills, extra squeezes of paint, etc., while the children work. When the music has finished stop work and assess the results. Younger children may want to stop here; older ones can now move from scrap paper to their final piece.

When everyone is ready again, play the piece as many times as is necessary, or requested, until the children have finished their work. As in all paintings, encourage filling all the paper with colour, just as Georgia O'Keeffe did in *Blue and Green Music*.

Further ideas (Reception–Year 6)

Interactive display   When displaying the work, add a copy of the recording and machine to play it on, plus some pastels and paper, so that other children can hear the music which inspired the paintings and have a go themselves.

Painting to other music   Try painting to other pieces of music, choosing pieces which evoke moods, such as 'Aquarium' or 'The Swan' from Saint-Saens' *Carnival of the Animals*, Gershwin's *Rhapsody in Blue* or the Montagues and Capulets theme (*Dance of the Knights*) from Prokofiev's *Romeo and Juliet*.

Music to paintings   Try the activity the other way round, looking at a painting and using it as inspiration to create a piece of music. Abstract work by artists such as Bridget Riley, Joan Miro and Paul Klée are ideal as they often have visible rhythms and mean that children cannot base their ideas on recognisable images, but almost any painting can be used as a stimulus for a musical composition.

Literacy

Three-prop stories

Story composition is notoriously difficult for some children. The ideas below offer simple structures; small 'hooks' on which children can hang a story, rather than be faced with a blank page and a blank mind!

Suitable for   Whole class, groups, pairs or individuals, Years 2–6.

You will need   A length of string; a coin; a cork; three other objects as props for your Machines story (see *Introduction*, below, for full explanation); scrap paper; writing books; pencils.

If you can get hold of any examples of writers'/artists'/musicians' preliminary work (scribblings, sketches, rejected ideas), they can prove an extremely valuable resource both for writing and artwork. You can often find these in biographies, which are worth borrowing from the library to show children. Thomas Hardy, Charlotte Brontë, Mozart, the Beatles, and Leonardo da Vinci all left behind examples of this kind, showing planning, corrections and rejections. The British Library in London sells postcards of some of these. Children may also have heard of or seen on television the detailed illustrated notebooks kept by J. K. Rowling as she planned the Harry Potter series. If you cannot find famous examples, a local writer or artist might be able to provide notes or sketches, or photocopies of them.

Introduction

Choose three objects for your Machines story beforehand (do not show them to the children yet) with the following in mind:

1   Objects which suit the subject of the story.

2   Objects which are relevant, but not restricting. For example, for a story about machines, a cogwheel, a spring and a can of oil would all be relevant, but are too restricted to an actual machine to offer scope for children's minds to diverge and imagine unusual twists or plot lines. One of these objects, plus two others less obviously related, would provide better stimulus.

3   Objects which can fulfil more than one function, again to exercise children's minds imaginatively. For example, a length of string could be used for measuring, tying something up, finding your way out of a labyrinth, strangling an enemy, hanging things on, etc., whereas a mobile phone is probably less versatile!

Explain that you are going to plan a story which somehow involves three objects. This would be a good point at which to talk about J.K. Rowling's planning notebooks, or show examples of writers' scribbled notes. Notice how these writers and artists did not throw these away, but valued them and kept them, luckily for us, so that they and we could see their thought processes and how they improved and developed their ideas.

Show the children the string, the coin and the cork. Use these to acquaint them with the idea of using objects to structure a story, and have a verbal practice run. How many ways can they think of in which these objects could be used? Write these on the board and then look for ways of linking some of them together. Don't take this story too far (unless it becomes so gripping that it is valuable to see it right through to the end!). The aim is to stop it once children get the idea and then move on to individual work on the main story.

The literacy activity

Introduce the three objects you have chosen to be props for the Machine story. Give the children scrap paper to make lists and jot down ideas: one piece of paper could be for writing down any thoughts about machines, and three more pieces could be used for thoughts on using the three props. Encourage divergent thinking about machines rather than starting from a fixed or stereotyped idea. A machine can be small, huge, easily available, rare, dangerous, safe to use at home, functioning correctly, out of control, ordinary, extraordinary . . . It can make, print, lift, press, fill, fasten, seal . . . Where is it sited? Who controls it? Is the controller the main character in the story, or is someone else?

Emphasise that the three objects should be integral to the storyline, not simply mentioned along the way. They are the hooks upon which the story is hung. An example of a way of incorporating a coin into a story might be that the hero is shot but the bullet hits the coin in his pocket, thus saving his life, as opposed to him spending it on sweets which then play no further part in the storyline.

A full session could be devoted to this planning, with the story being written up to a week later. This often gives children time to dwell on their initial ideas so that they look forward to writing their story rather than having to think it up on the spur of the moment.

Further ideas (Key Stage 2)

Other three-prop methods

Try building a story in a similar way using the following, either chosen beforehand by the teacher, or chosen by the child for his/her own story:

1   Three sounds;
2   Three smells;
3   One object, one location, one emotion (e.g. supermarket trolley, pier, revenge);
4   Three phrases (e.g. 'furious scrambling', 'a sight beyond belief', 'felt calmer for a moment'. Sometimes I take these randomly from books children are reading.);

5   Title, first line, last line (e.g. 'The Disastrous Machine'/It was not often that Bernard went to the cinema, but today had been different from the start./Never again would he make the same mistake.).

All these form a useful lead to help children devise the three props which all stories need – beginning, middle and end.

Chapter 8

Creation

Exploring life in all its forms, its vast variety on earth, and the place of humans within it, is essential to children's understanding of themselves and their environment. From the birth of new siblings and pets to watching a bean seed sprout, they are surrounded by evidence of ongoing creation in their daily lives. The lesson plans below offer opportunities for children to discover and celebrate the difficulties and beauty of life on earth.

Drama

'Running the Zoo'

There is more to a zoo than meets the eye – and this drama is designed to show children the importance of planning, liaising and teamwork in running a large enterprise in which animals are the focal point.

Suitable for   Whole class, Years 4–6, possibly Year 3. For drama suited to younger children, see *Further ideas* below.

You will need

1   As much information as possible from a zoo, in the form of leaflets, brochures, maps, tourist guides, etc. If you have a local zoo which children may know, use this, but if not contact any large zoo (visit <www.zoos.bizland.com> for a list of UK zoos and contact details). You can also ask to speak to the Education Officer who may be able to give you further details about aspects of the zoo.
2   A set of character cards. There are eight provided on the photocopiable pages which follow, but you may wish to make your own to suit the zoo you are using or the reading level of the class. Cut one of each – mounted on card they will last a bit longer!
3   Peel-off labels bearing the job title found on each card are useful – making four of each title will give you enough for a class of 32.
4   Chairs (optional)

Introduction

Prior to the session, display maps around the work space (enough for all children to see one clearly) showing the layout of the zoo. Introduce the topic by explaining that you have been in touch with the zoo, and show them the literature you have been sent. Go through some of this with the class, pointing out any particular features of the zoo such as guided tours, animal adoption schemes or awards it may have won. Once an interest has been generated, invite the children to spend some time looking at the leaflets and going round the room familiarising themselves with the layout of the zoo.

Keepers

You look after the animals every day in all kinds of weather, and sometimes at night. You need to know exactly what each animal can eat, how they behave and what they need. You also keep records of their health and behaviour.

Transport Staff

You are in charge of all the vehicles used in the zoo. You have to drive the right food to the animals, drive visitors on the tour bus and sometimes move animals to a different place.

Garden Staff

You look after the trees, bushes and flowers in the park areas. Some of the plants are grown as food for the animals. You have to know which these are and how much to grow and gather. You also grow some rare and exotic plants needed for the habitat of certain creatures.

Works Staff

You are responsible for all the odd jobs around the zoo. You build and mend animal houses, so you have to know exactly what kind of home each species needs and that they are safe and secure. You carry out all necessary repairs.

Veterinary Staff

You check each animal regularly and attend to any which are ill. If an animal dies you are responsible for finding out why. You need to check that the zoo is a healthy place and is caring for its animals properly.

Catering Staff

You run the cafés, restaurants and food kiosks around the zoo. You have to make sure there is enough food and drink ordered for the number of tourists. Sometimes you have to organise food for a big event such as a conference or if filming is taking place.

Office Staff

You keep careful records of all the animals – where and when the zoo got them, and the animal adoption scheme. You also answer the phone, letters and emails, dealing politely with enquiries, problems or complaints.

Education Staff

You make information sheets and workcards for children and school parties who visit the zoo. You have to plan activities and give talks to help children learn about the zoo. You also teach them about saving rare animals and looking after the environment.

The drama

Divide the children into eight groups. Explain that to run a zoo or any similar venture smoothly, many people are needed, each responsible for a different area of work. Hand out one character card to each group (you may like to give some thought to which card suits which group!) and give them some time to read the information and discuss their responsibilities. To help clarify these, ask the group to imagine their way through a typical day in their work roles. What is the first thing they do on arrival? What is the busiest time of their day? Where do they eat? What everyday occurrences could they expect?

Now ask the children to go into the role on their character card, bringing the zoo to life. Go round the room constantly, checking that the children are on task and giving them jobs to do. Have the Works Staff noticed that gap in the wallaby enclosure? Are the Catering Staff aware that fifteen school parties are booked for lunch tomorrow?

After a while bring the children back to sit down and give out the peel-off labels, which they should wear so that everyone can see who does what job. Ask a spokesperson from each group to explain their group's responsibilities clearly to the whole class. Point out to the children that these groups all depend on one another and that the zoo could not function unless all the groups liaise. Ask them to go back into role, but this time to start some networking between the groups. For example, the Vets might need to ask the Transport Staff to move a sick animal into temporary accommodation, or the Office Staff might have received a complaint about litter and have to suggest to the Catering Staff that they put up notices around the bins near the café.

When the networking has continued for a suitable length of time, ask the children to sit in their groups and come up with a problem that they might encounter in their daily work. Encourage the children to consider what realistic problems might actually arise, rather than an elephant escaping and rampaging through the restaurant, etc. When they are ready, ask each group to choose a spokesperson to bring the problem to the zoo staff's monthly board meeting. At this point, to make the meeting feel more formal, you can put chairs out in a circle.

The teacher can now take on the role of chairman/woman, asking the first spokesperson to bring their problem to the meeting. Anyone may contribute, and the aim is to solve the problem. Encourage lively discussion and practical ideas. I often find that humour and accusations play a part in such meetings too, and these must be steered as the chairman thinks fit! Make sure that each spokesperson has a chance to air their problem. If time permits, children can physically act out rectifying the problems.

To bring the drama to a close, make sure that children have grasped that the zoo needs a wide range of people and skills to make it function, and that these people must support and work tactfully with one another, just as they must in a school.

Further ideas (Reception–Year 3)

Noah's ark A version of the above for younger children. Choose two children to be Mr and Mrs Noah. Divide the rest of the class into six groups. Each group needs a leader – Shem, Ham, Japhet, Mrs Shem, Mrs Ham and Mrs Japhet. Noah decides which species the three son's groups are responsible for and Mrs Noah decides for the wives. The groups then set to work building the part of the ark their animals will live in, preparing its food and bedding, etc., with Mr and Mrs Noah checking that the cheetahs are not next to the rabbits and so on. They then hold a meeting at which each group reports a problem which Mr and Mrs Noah try to solve. Play a tape of heavy rain or stormy music. Each group then leads their creatures on board and the ark sails away.

Dance

Hatching birds

This short dance is ideal for young children and tells the story of a baby bird hatching and learning to fly.

Suitable for   Whole class, Reception and Year 1.

You will need   Choreographed music: 'Volières' (or 'Aviaries') from *The Carnival of the Animals* by Camille Saint-Saens. Suggested alternative music: anything cheerful, trilling and bird-like, but as the Saint-Saens is well-known and readily available finding an alternative should not be necessary. A photograph of a chick hatching from its egg makes a very useful starting point.

Introduction

Show the children the photograph of the baby bird hatching. Why is it wet? Explain that the bird's first meal is the egg yolk, which it eats when it is still inside the egg, and which gives it enough energy to push out of the eggshell. It has a special egg tooth to break the shell with, which falls off later. It is a great effort for the baby bird to hatch and its feathers dry once it is outside.

Ask the children what skills the bird will have to learn. Ideas might include flying, finding food, finding somewhere to rest.

The dance

0.00   Children lie in their own space on their backs, legs bent up, clasping their knees to their chests as tightly as possible, with eyes closed up, to represent the bird in the egg.

0.05   First struggle – still clasping their legs, children begin to wiggle slightly on their backs, their facial expressions showing that they are trying to push their way out of the egg.

0.10   Second struggle – in same position, still with eyes shut, children wiggle their bottoms more determinedly.

0.15   Third struggle – children roll from side to side a little in an effort to get out of the egg.

0.20   Fourth struggle – children hammer with their 'eggtooth' (actually their nose!) on the shell.

0.26   The eggshell breaks. Children suddenly sit up, necks tall, eyes popped open, arms (wings) closely by their sides.

0.31   Get up and have a little shake to get dry.

0.36   Baby birds realise that they have wings, look at them in amazement, and stretch them out luxuriantly with a big smile.

0.41   Turn round on the spot to show off new stretched wings.

0.46   The theme tune returns – all baby birds fly around space. Encourage light, tiptoeing feet, no touching another bird allowed and a feeling of a first tentative flight – rather than zooming around furiously.

0.51   Stop in a space, put wings behind back, bend face down and make pecking movements with head.

0.56   Still with wings folded behind back and body leaning slightly forward, use feet to scratch earth. There is time for about three scratches with the right foot and then three with the left.

1.01   All turn on the spot with wings out.

1.06   Fly to another space.

1.09   Perch on a branch, wings folded behind back.

1.21   As the music ends tuck head down sideways, close eyes and give a sleepy smile.

Further ideas (Reception–Year 6)

Other animal dances   Several of the other pieces which make up Saint-Saens' *Carnival of the Animals* lend themselves well to contrasting animal dances for young children, particularly 'Aquarium', 'Hens and Cocks', and 'Kangaroos'. Older children will appreciate the humour of 'Tortoises' and the sensitivity of 'The Swan', and teachers might like to use these for Key Stage 2 dance.

Creation dances   The biblical version of the Creation story (Genesis 1 v.1–2 v.3) was my starting point for a series of six dances, one by each class in a school, each representing one day of God's work.

Day 1   Light, Year 3 (Rautavaara's Fifth Symphony)
Day 2   Heaven, Years 1–2 ('In Paradisum' from Fauré's *Requiem*)
Day 3   Seas, Dry Land and Plants, Year 4 ('Sunday Morning' from Britten's *Four Sea Interludes*)
Day 4   Sun, Moon and Stars, Year 5 (*Two Fanfares* by John Adams)
Day 5   Birds and Fish, Reception–Year 1 ('Volières' and 'Aquarium' from *The Carnival of the Animals* by Saint-Saens)
Day 6   Creatures, including humans, Year 6, (Afro-Celt Sound System, Volume 2, *Release It*, CD RW76 7243 8 47324 2 4).

Art

Ceramic fish

As clay is earth, one of the earliest materials in creation, it is well suited to the topic. Ceramic fish proved to be a very exciting and successful project with children in Reception, Years 1 and 2, and suits any age range. The use of paint-on, non-firing metallic glazes and nail varnish gave the fishes a wonderful shimmer!

Suitable for   A group, or a whole class working in groups, Reception–Year 6.

You will need   Clay – buff stoneware, available cheaply from school catalogues, is best as it fires to a very pale colour, making the glazes show up well. One 10kg bag will make two to three large fish. Photographs of all kinds of fish; pencils; scrap paper; unscented handcream; clay mats; wooden rollers and lengths of dowel for roller guides (optional); old tea towels or pieces of cotton cloth; wooden skewer; blunt or plastic knife (for teacher's use); old paintbrushes; cocktail sticks; newspaper; glazes (see end of this section for supplier).

Introduction

Allow time for the children to look at the photographs of fish, noticing their body and tail shapes, position and number of fins, their eyes, scales and colours.

Give each child a pencil and scrap paper and ask them to draw a simple fish shape showing body, fins, tail and eye only, and not to write their name. Collect the papers in and explain that we are going to design clay fish incorporating the features we choose from the drawings. The class can do this together or the teacher can take the decision, but the aim is to decide on the best body shape, the best top fin, etc. Put the chosen drawings aside.

Note: Before beginning, measure the size of the kiln shelf so that you do not make the fish too big for the kiln! The fishes made by my class measured about 40 × 26cm.

The art activity

Children should rub a small amount of handcream into their hands before you give them each a piece of clay about the size of a tangerine, which they should then wedge. Wedging is essential if the clay is to be fired, as it removes air bubbles which could blow open in the kiln. To wedge correctly, knock the clay with the heel of the hand (do not smack with the palm) and keep turning the clay constantly until it is knocked into a dense ball.

Children should place their ball in the middle of their mat and either roll it out to just under a centimetre in thickness using the rollers and guides, or press it slowly and evenly down all over with the heel of their hand to the required thickness. The balls of clay should now look like roundish biscuits.

Place an old tea towel on a table and put the clay discs on it. The discs should slightly overlap and you should use only as many as you need to make up the size and vague shape of the final fish. Use spare discs to make more fish at the same time.

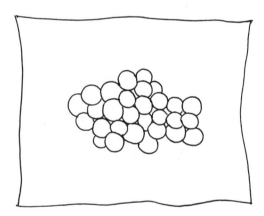

Figure 15 Clay discs laid in place

The children should now carefully merge all the discs together into one large, flat piece by smearing the higher overlapping parts of the discs into the lower ones. Keep the thickness to just under a centimetre and as even as possible – if it gets too thin, smear in some spare clay. You may like to finish by lightly rolling the piece with a roller, although the surface is not going to show.

Using the chosen drawings, mark the body, fins, tail and eye *lightly* on to the flat piece of clay with a wooden skewer. It is appropriate if this is done by the children who designed the chosen features. If they go wrong they can wipe out the line with a finger and draw it again.

The teacher can now cut out the fish shape with a blunt or plastic knife. Save cut-off clay for the slip (liquid clay) and decorations, below. If you plan to mount the fish by putting screws or nails through it, use the wooden skewer at this point to make clear, clean holes where you need them.

(If you have not time to continue working on the fish, cover it with a plastic bin bag and return to it in the next 24 hours.)

Children can now add decoration to the fish by rolling thin sausages for the ribs of fins and tail, making an eye, and pressing small flattened circles for scales. Each must be joined correctly to the body of the fish with slip. To make slip, stir one drop of water onto a spare blob of clay with an old paintbrush until it is creamy. Crosshatch (scratch roughly) the two surfaces to be joined (e.g. body and scale), poke the slip into the scratches with a brush and push firmly together.

To give a 3-dimensional look to the fish, peel part of it carefully from the cloth and put some small pads of newspaper under the main body section to give it a domed shape. Do not overstuff – make sure that the edges of the body touch the cloth all the way round. This newspaper can be left in place as it will burn off in the kiln.

Leave the fish to dry thoroughly at room temperature before firing to 1000 degrees.

To glaze the fish, my class used bottled glazes and fired them in the usual way, but left some scales and ribs unglazed. On these we used non-firing glazes which have a metallic shimmer. (See below for supplier.) We also painted some of the scales with a selection of blue, green and purple nail varnishes. Finally the fish were mounted on boards which the children painted dark blue.

Figure 16 The shapes of the fish as designed by some of the children

Further ideas (Reception–Year 6)

Shoal Children can make their own smaller individual fish and these can be displayed together in one large shoal.

Clay creations Many other aspects of Creation can be explored through clay, such as moonscapes, birds/other animals, underwater seascape with weeds and shells, and human figures.

Supplier of glazes Potterycrafts Ltd, Winton House, 2 Winton Approach, Watford Road, Croxley Green, Rickmansworth, Herts WD3 3TL. Tel. 01923 800006. Wide range of glazes and all pottery equipment, and good practical advice. <http://www.potterycrafts.co.uk>

Literacy

This week's news

A chance for children to write the Creation story in newspaper form. There are many versions of the Creation myth from different faiths and cultures which you can use for this project, but the biblical version is well suited as it is neatly divided into seven days of news.

Suitable for Whole class divided into groups, Years 4–6. See *Further ideas*, below, for activities for younger children.

You will need The Creation story from the Bible (Genesis 1 v.1–2 v.3). The Revised English Bible is a useful version for children. It is helpful to make seven cards, divide the story into seven days and stick one day's events on each card. Examples of (suitable!) stories from newspapers; paper; pencils; camera if you wish to include photographs in your newspaper.

Introduction

Look at some of the newspaper stories, drawing attention to their format (headlines, sub-headings, length of paragraphs, reported speech, style, etc.). Discuss what makes news. What parts of a story are important, relevant and irrelevant? What makes a good story? What makes a good newspaper?

Now ask a child to read out Genesis 1 vv.1–5. By any standards, this is fairly startling news! How would a newspaper have handled such an event? Obviously there were no humans around to write a report, and children may like to debate who the writers and readers of this newspaper are – or they may be content to accept that it is an imaginary, if impossible, situation. Ask other children to read out the remaining six days' events.

The literacy activity

Divide the children into seven groups of journalists. Give each group one of the seven cards with one day's Creation news. Each group's task is to write a page on their day's news, but the class's task as a whole is to produce a newspaper covering the whole week. This means that they will need to liaise with each other to ensure continuity and similarity of style, and avoid contradictions. For example, the opening sentence of Day Four might be: 'Following our report yesterday on the amazing appearance of a liquid substance known as water, we can now inform readers that this is now illuminated by a spherical structure which has appeared above the earth . . .'

Obviously children will write at their own level, but should try to echo the style of a newspaper report. To avoid leaders taking over their groups, allot different tasks to group members or pairs, such as writer, editor, photographer, reporter at the scene, etc. Some could be responsible for suggesting headlines and dividing the writing into subheadings.

Photographs can be included in the report and children will need to decide how to set up suitable scenes for photographing, using props, painted scenery, real plants, etc.

Remember that if journalists were writing at the time they would not know how many days the Creation was going to take, so the writers for Day Seven will be the bearers of the perhaps unexpected news that the Creation has come to an end. Other day's writers can speculate on the topic: 'The astounding events of the last few days show no sign of abating . . . we are left pondering on whether still more wonders will reveal themselves', and so on.

While there may well be some element of humour in such a project, care should be taken to show respect for the subject matter also, and to encourage children to convey to readers the awe, beauty and splendour of all around us, whatever our beliefs as to how it came about.

Further ideas (Reception–Year 6)

Creation I Spy (Reception–Year 2)   Using the illustration (Figure 17), ask children to find one or more items in the picture for each initial letter given at the foot of the picture. Children can then draw their own pictures and write the initial letters of some of the items they have drawn. They then swap pictures with a friend and see if they can spot the right items. If their drawings prove too hard to identify they can cut pictures from magazines and make a creation collage with written letters beside it.

Creation instructions (Years 1–6)   An exercise to help children to follow and to give clear verbal instructions and clear written instructions. The teacher begins by giving verbal instructions one by one which children must follow to draw a creation picture. (It is better to prepare these beforehand rather than try to make them up as you go along!) These instructions will differ according to the age of the children, but an example might be:

1   Draw a flower with six petals, a stalk and two long leaves in the exact middle of your paper.
2   Behind the flower there is a tree with a thick trunk and large, spreading branches.
3   Towards the top of the trunk there is a large, oval hole.
4   In the hole four toadstools are growing.
5   To the left of the tree a rabbit is sitting looking at the flower, (etc.).

You can ask children to volunteer to give verbal instructions to the class for a very simple creation picture, or to write their own instructions and see if the class can follow them.

b t g s c r f d

Figure 17

Chapter 9

Feelings

Every moment of every person's day is filled with emotion of one kind or another. These emotions are often brought about by the actions of others, and in turn dictate our own behaviour. Understanding the feelings of others and how our behaviour affects them is a vital and lifelong learning skill which is essential to personal and social development. The following lessons explore different emotional areas and seek to address the issues to which they may give rise.

Drama

'Village Unrest'

Drama is the ideal learning medium through which to explore emotion, but a clear focus is essential. Here, difficulties in a small community form the basis of a realistic drama giving children the opportunity to use social skills they will need throughout life. The drama can easily be held in the classroom.

Suitable for   Whole class, Years 4–6, possibly able Year 3.

You will need   Peel-off labels and pen; chairs; a fictitious map, large enough to be clearly seen by all, showing a village with features such as those shown in Figure 18 and including an obvious problem area, in this case the chemical plant. Please note that the illustration serves only as an example. You may prefer to show alternative problem areas such as 'site of proposed road widening/bridge/traffic calming/skateboard park', etc.

Introduction

Introduce the map to the class and spend some time getting to know the features and layout. What kind of a place would this be to live in? Does it have good facilities? What might its good and bad points be? Decide on the focus problem that the village is facing.

Who would live in this village? List with the children all the residents who are likely to form this community, using the features of the map as clues. The list might include schoolchildren, housewives, retired people, a farmer, hairdresser, grocer, café owner, vet, teacher, school caretaker, park attendant, refuse collectors, river warden, doctor, etc.

Each child should then be allotted a role as a member of this community. It is wise for the teacher to have a hand in this rather than giving children a totally free choice; for example, a maximum of two should take on the role of schoolchildren, and these roles must be the children's actual age or above. Children who may naturally choose to contribute little should be given a role which, while non-threatening, requires them to have a definite viewpoint, while children who have good leadership ability (as opposed to show-offs!) can be given a role of key importance in the discussion. Ensure that the roles are clear and not nebulous (for example, '10-year-

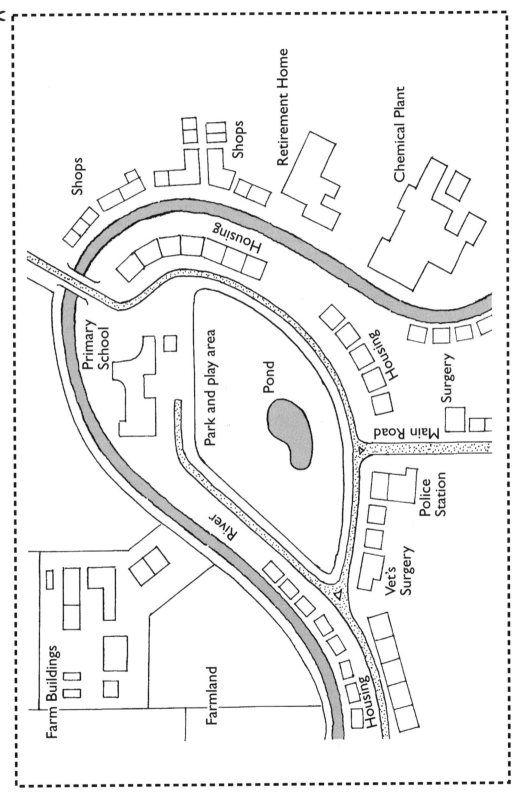

Figure 18

old schoolgirl' or 'retired nurse' rather than 'schoolchild' or 'old lady') and that their views are all likely to have a bearing on the problem. Each child should then wear a peel-off label to show their role.

Now allow time for children to consider their viewpoint on the problem. How is it affecting them? What do they think is causing it/are changes necessary? Have they any evidence to bring to the meeting? Some children may want to put together a body of evidence with others; for instance, a group of retired people may have formed a rota for observing traffic flow, or the doctor and vet might have collated information on ailments they have recently dealt with.

Chairs give a more realistic and formal feeling to the drama and should be set out as if for a meeting.

The drama

The teacher (or, if working with older children, a very capable child, with the teacher to support) explains that he/she is here to chair a meeting of the village Residents' Association to discuss the issue at the forefront of everyone's mind, the allegations of river pollution (or proposed motorway, or whatever your chosen problem is). The drama takes the form of a discussion and must be carefully steered by the chairperson. At all times it should be kept as realistic as possible. Points to ensure are that:

- every person's view is heard, preferably in fairly equal measure;
- only one person speaks at once;
- all remarks are made through the chair;
- discussion is kept to opinions and evidence, and is not allowed to deteriorate into anecdote or chatting;
- it is understood by all that the chairperson is in sole charge.

It is possible for this drama to become very personal and occasionally quite heated, just as in a real meeting. In one school the class became so involved that the drama continued for four sessions, and in another a child playing the role of a farmer, whose real father worked in the chemical industry brought in some safely sealed substances claiming that these were river samples he had taken from his farmland and had analysed!

Further ideas (Reception–Year 6)

ABC, 1–10 This is an exercise to help children convey feelings by focusing on the feeling itself and not on subject matter. Children work in pairs. They have a conversation together but can only use the names of letters or numbers in their speech. Their feelings must be put over through their voice, manner and body language – laughter, whispering, being moody, etc. Children may at first find this difficult or embarrassing, so it is best not to observe them too closely and not to ask a pair to show their work to the rest of the group until it has been practised over a number of sessions. Sometimes children can become so adept at this that it is possible for onlookers to guess at the subject matter of their conversation, and I once witnessed two 5-year-old girls, one being upset and the other with her arm around her, murmuring '1, 2, 3' in a comforting tone.

Dance

Injustice

This dance was created to explore the feelings associated with different kinds of injustice and focused particularly on the people of Africa. The children's ideas came from news reports they had watched on television.

Suitable for Whole class, Key Stage 2, particularly the older children.

You will need Choreographed music: Track 1, 'Adiemus', from *Songs of Sanctuary* by Karl Jenkins. Suggested alternative music: other tracks from this or subsequent 'Adiemus' albums, African chants or African-inspired music such as Paul Simon's *Graceland* or Afro-Celt Sound System's Volume 2 (for details see *Further ideas* at the end of Creation – Dance). Newspaper articles and photographs relating to issues of injustice in Africa are useful to get initial thoughts going.

Introduction

Using the newspaper articles and the children's own knowledge as a starting point, discuss the differences between life in Africa (or one part of Africa) and our own country, particularly those things which we take for granted. When I carried out this project with a Year 6 class the issues raised included working conditions, food, shelter, refugees and racial tension, but also the beauty of the country, its traditions and its wildlife. While discussing the positive side, one aspect which hit us was the readiness of the African people to rejoice, praise and show gratitude for every blessing (such as rain), compared to our own reserved and complaining attitude. A comment which struck hard came from a young African visitor who spoke at my church. She remarked on how astonished she was on seeing the gloomy faces of British people standing at bus stops or doing their shopping. Spreading her hands in incredulity she said, 'I look at them and I think, "Why are you not smiling or dancing? You have food!"'

The children I worked with then developed movements which would convey all these ideas and built them into the following dance. It is easily adaptable to your own class's ideas.

The dance

Before the dance, children sit in groups of three or four, one group of three in the middle of the space and the remaining groups around the central group. Each group sits in a circle facing inwards with heads bowed, and remaining still. The children in the middle group do not sit but squat, balancing on balls of feet with hands on the floor and heads bowed.

0.00 On the sung introductory phrase all children remain still except the middle group, which represents the sun rising. They slowly rise from their squatting position as smoothly as possible while pressing their palms to join with the palm of the child next to them. As they rise they lift their joined hands to form three high peaks between them and then release their hands and spread them out like the sun's rays. This entire movement should be timed to take up the 10 second introductory phrase.

0.10 As the rhythmic theme begins, all children move to bring the land to life, the aim being to convey a baking heatwave. Individuals, groups or pairs can decide how best to show this, shimmering their hands, bending their backs under the heat, covering their heads with their hands, spreading out their arms and legs like the rays of the sun, etc. The space should become filled with weaving, slow, interacting shapes and forms.

0.29 The theme is repeated and there is a change in the movement pattern, as despite the heat the people toil and work. In contrast to **0.10**, the class I worked with now used the rhythm to dig, plough, drag, lift or chop, repeating their chosen movement sequence several times to symbolise the relentlessness of labour.

0.47 At the key change/choral singing, all the children form a large circle. This part of the dance shows thanksgiving for shelter and water, and requires one leader to make symbolic and smooth movements which the others copy so that the whole circle moves together. Ideas from our dance included making a peak with the hands over the head, slowly kneeling down, miming picking up a large waterpot and placing it on the head, and rising smoothly.

1.14 A solo is now played on the quena (an instrument which sounds similar to a recorder) and the children form pairs. Some pairs represent the jungle and some the animals within it. The jungle pairs should be as imaginative as possible in creating twisted plant forms for the creatures to creep through, but they must be able to hold these positions still until the quena music finishes.

1.50 As the chorus sings again, children form into groups to represent queues of refugees, walking endlessly in a large circle, carrying burdens, stooping, supporting each other, etc.

2.07 Key change – use this time to move smoothly back into original groups as at start of dance. All groups sit facing inwards in their individual circles.

2.17 The Adiemus theme starts again. The children in my dance developed their own movements to this section, which they saw as a time of prayer for help. Some made classic praying movements, raising their hands and faces, bowing, etc., while others developed rhythmic mantras of movement, holding hands and moving them to and fro or round and round. Each group came up with something different and managed to generate a powerful feeling of reverence. As throughout the whole dance, facial expression is very important here and must convey sincerity of feeling.

2.34 At the key change/chorus, all rise smoothly and walk gradually into two long lines, one down each side of the working space and facing each other.

2.51 Slowly the lines move towards each other. When they meet, conflict ensues. Children devised slow motion fighting, accusing and defending movements with their opposite partner for this sequence, using facial expression and eye contact but never actually touching them.

3.02 There is a long wind-down until the music ends at **3.51**. The fighting can gradually break down, opposite pairs gradually turning away from each other and slowly walking into the two long lines again. The dance ends with all children in the lines, backs turned and heads bowed.

Further ideas (Key Stage 2)

Exploring other countries through dance – see the Dance sections in the History, Journeys, and Rainforest chapters.

Starting with music An obvious starting point for dance on the theme of feelings is music which has been written to specifically convey a particular emotion. Examples include:

> Holst *The Planets* ('Mars' – War; 'Venus' – Peace; 'Jupiter' – Jollity)
> Elgar *Sospiri* (Sighs)
> Dvorak *Humoresque* (Humour)
> Rautavaara 'Melancholy' from *Cantus Arcticus*
> Other suitable examples can be found in the dance sections of previous chapters.

Art

Lonely shapes

An exploration of colour and mood for Key Stage 1 children using a poem and a painting as inspiration. The work also addresses positive ways to help lonely people.

Suitable for   Whole class or group, Reception, Years 1 and 2.

You will need   A copy of the poem *When I'm Lonely*, below; a reproduction of *Whistler's Mother*, painted in 1871 by James Whistler; large sheets of white paper; brushes; paints; mixing plates or trays; waterpots.

Introduction

Look at the painting of Whistler's mother with the children. Discuss how she is feeling and what clues there are to suggest that she is feeling unhappy (such as the handkerchief she is holding). She is sitting down – but is she comfortable and relaxed? What is she remembering or thinking about?

Talk about the colours the artist has used in the painting and why he might have chosen them. (Whistler gave this portrait an alternative title: *Study in Grey and Black*.)

Read the poem to the children once or twice.

> *When I'm Lonely*
> When I'm lonely
> My body doesn't want to move
> It stays still
> With heavy eyes and a sad throat.
> There must be lots of smiles inside me
> But I can't make them work.
> My head hangs down
> Full of wishes that won't come true.

What do the poem and the painting have in common? Ask the children to describe how they feel when they are lonely. Is it the same as being alone? The poem says 'my body doesn't want to move'. How would the lady in the painting move? Ask the children to imagine they are her, and mime drinking a cup of tea or turning the pages of a letter. Talk about other phrases in the poem. What causes us to feel lonely?

Ensure that discussions of this kind lead to a positive conclusion. What we can do if someone is feeling lonely? Ask if any of the children can give an example of a time when someone has helped them feel less lonely, or a time they have helped someone else. Invite the children to speak to the lady in the painting – what would they say to make her feel better? (For related ideas see Paintings – Literacy).

The art activity

Encourage the children to experiment with colour mixing to create 'lonely' colours. Try adding minute quantities of black to other colours to dull them, or small quantities of blue or brown.

Ask them to use some of these colours to create a 'lonely' painting. This need not necessarily show a person – it could be an arrangement of shapes and colours which express loneliness. Discuss where shapes should be placed on the paper – for example, a grey, flat blob right in the corner, or a small blue dot alone in the middle. If there is more than one lonely shape on the paper, this could lead to further discussion. Couldn't the two lonely people get together? Do they know about each other? Perhaps when we are lonely, we think a bit too much about ourselves – maybe there is someone who needs us.

Discuss ways in which these shapes could be made less lonely. With clean brushes and water, invite the children to experiment with 'cheering up' colours. Use these to add other shapes to the paper. In what ways could these shapes be different from the lonely shapes? Where will they be placed on the paper?

Further ideas (Reception–Year 6)

Shapes to show feelings   Following the above activity, show children examples of work by artists who used shapes to convey ideas in their paintings, such as Miro, Malevich and Kandinsky.

Class display   Try the art activity in a representational way by asking one child to draw or paint a lonely person and everyone else to draw or paint ways in which the person could be helped – playing games, sharing food, talking, comforting, etc. Make a large display with the lonely drawing in the centre surrounded by the other pictures. Very young or less able children can make a similar display by cutting pictures from magazines showing families eating together, children playing and so on.

More poem/painting combinations   The following poems and paintings are useful to address other emotions:

Excitement   Poem: *From a Railway Carriage* by Robert Louis Stevenson
Painting: *Train Landscape* by Eric Ravilious, 1941

Peace   Poem: *Summer Afternoon* by A.A. Milne
Painting: *Salisbury Cathedral* by John Constable, 1823

Anger   Poem: *The Quarrel* by Eleanor Farjeon
Painting: *Fighting Forms* by Franz Marc, 1914

Literacy

Letters

Letters can be fascinating, providing facts, information, clues, evidence and an insight into people's thoughts. This literacy activity is designed to stimulate children to want to read a text (in this case Shakespeare's *A Midsummer Night's Dream*) by allowing them to explore letters from the characters. It can be adapted to suit any book or play.

Suitable for   Whole class or groups, Years 4–6.

You will need   Photocopies (one per child) of two or three previously prepared letters relating to your chosen text (details below); pencils and paper.

Introduction

The idea of this activity is that it is an introduction to a text which children have never read and which should not be mentioned by the teacher at all until either (a) the children guess or (b) they demand to know more!

Talk with the class about why people write letters. Before the telephone they were almost the only form of communication, other than speech, so they were of great importance. Now we have much faster methods, yet vast amounts are still sent through the postal system.

Discuss the advantages of letters. An email may seem impersonal and the writer may feel uneasy about expressing emotion on a computer. There is something very personal about handwriting which is lost in type – it has a closeness and shows the writer has spent time thinking of the recipient. There is also an element of excitement in receiving a letter through the post – a secret sealed in an envelope – which is absent in emails or phone calls, although these may be special too.

People sometimes find it hard to express their feelings in speech to someone else. It may be that it is too difficult to say what they want to say while face to face with the other person. Perhaps they think the other person will interrupt or that an argument will ensue. Or perhaps they fear that it will all 'come out wrong', and so they need to clarify their thoughts. Letter writing solves all these problems; so often feelings are more readily and clearly expressed in letters.

The literacy activity

Explain that we are now going to look closely at some letters written by different people about the same thing, and see what we can learn about the situation from what they say.

Prepare two or three letters giving the views of different characters in the text. Figures 19, 20 and 21 are three examples relating to *A Midsummer Night's Dream*, Act I, scene 1. It is interesting to note how closely the antics of Shakespeare's lovers resemble a television soap, and it is this similarity which I find gains children's interest.

Children should be given plenty of time to read all these letters and discuss them in pairs or groups, noting down their findings. All groups should then report back to the class. Only after this has been done and interest aroused should the play be introduced to answer questions and to find out what happens.

Further ideas (Years 4–6)

Continue letter writing   Having begun to explore the text, children can now write further letters. Ideas might include:

- writing the replies to the original letters;
- writing subsequent letters from the original writers giving further news;
- writing letters from other characters in the play.

Diaries   These are another example of personal feelings in written form. Children can try writing a page from Hermia's, Puck's or Bottom's diary. See also History – Literacy for Guy Fawkes' diary and Stories – Literacy for related ideas.

My dear friend,

   I feel I must write to apologise for what you had to witness earlier today. It was wrong of me to offload my family problems on to you, especially in front of your fiancée. I hope you can both forgive me. But I'm afraid I feel very strongly about it, and I was grateful that you backed me up.

  Of course I don't want to send Hermia to a nunnery, or to die – she is my daughter and very dear to me. But the thought of her spending her life with that lovesick young fool Lysander, when she could marry the man I chose for her is simply too much to bear. And as for what that stupid boy said to him about marrying me – the cheek of it!

  Anyway, I've done it now. I've said she must decide by the new moon, and I'll have to stick to my word. You were both there and heard me say it – but I must say I'm dreading her reply.

  Luckily you too have no such problems. You look so happy and I very much look forward to your wedding. Let's hope things in my family are resolved by then.

     Sincerely,

      Egeus.

Figure 19

Dear Auntie,

Things have come to a head since I last wrote. I'm still in love with Hermia and that won't change. But earlier today her father turned pretty nasty, and in front of Theseus too. He actually said that if Hermia doesn't agree to marry that wretched Demi by the next full moon he will send her away either to die or be a nun! He wasn't joking either. He went on and on about how marvellous D. is until I said that maybe he should marry him! You should have seen his face! I stood my ground but it was quite unpleasant.

Auntie, I must ask a big favour of you. You know what Hermia means to me and you've put up with my letters for so long. H. and I have simply got to escape this situation. Can we possibly come to you? We plan to meet tomorrow night, so could be with you some time after that. We can then marry as soon as possible and put all this behind us.

I know this is a huge thing to ask, but we have no-one else to turn to and I am relying on your support. Besides, I long for you to meet Hermia at last — when you do, I'm sure you'll understand why I can't live without her.

With my love always,

L.

Figure 20

Dear Helena,

Thankyou so much for listening to me yesterday — you are such a good friend and I'll soon be far away and then Demi will be all yours! I can't think what he sees in me when I've made it so obvious that it's Ly I love and not him. And Ly made it pretty clear yesterday too! I was so proud of him! Dad was furious but Ly just calmly said "I'm just as good as Demi and what's more I love Hermia and she loves me."

I do too — oh, I can't wait to get to that wood tomorrow night — but keep it quiet, won't you? Only you know our secret plans and I know I can trust you.

I just can't believe that very soon my darling Ly will be my husband instead of having to sing under my window and bring me presents — mind you, I hope he'll carry on doing that! Thank goodness for his aunt — she's a life saver.

Bye for now, my very dear H. I wish that soon you may be as happy as Ly and I are. I'm absolutely sure D. is meant for you — it's just that he hasn't realised it yet!

Lots of love
Hermia
x

Figure 21

Chapter 10

Stories

Stories are a source of inspiration for many areas of the curriculum, and below are used as starting points for the four activities. See Feelings – Literacy, for a strategy for stimulating children to read a story, and Machines – Literacy for a story-writing format.

Drama

A television broadcast

An opportunity for children to create their own TV presentation featuring characters from books.

Suitable for   Whole class divided into groups, Key Stage 2, although the idea can be adapted for Key Stage 1 (see *Further ideas*, below).

You will need   One or more copies of a story well-known to all the class, perhaps one you have just finished reading to them, or one you are studying together (such as a Shakespeare play); pencils and paper; optional additions to make the broadcast more realistic (depending on how far you want to take it) such as a video camera, music to introduce and finish, desk, background logo, microphones, etc.

Introduction

Talk with the class about the format of a television broadcast featuring famous people. What might be included? What would viewers want to see? Ideas might include:

- narrator or 'link person' to introduce different sections of the programme;
- interviewer in studio with the famous people;
- roving reporter interviewing those known to the people;
- guest panel invited to discuss the people.

Divide the class into groups of between 4 and 8. Explain that each group is going to put together a broadcast about one or more of the characters from the story you have chosen.

How much time you allow for the preparation of the broadcast depends on how polished you (or the children) want it to be. It could be done as a presentation exercise within one lesson, or cover several lessons and end in a performance to others. The groups need to plan their broadcast and choose a role for each member of the group. Suggest that they write a script for the presenter of the programme, plan the interviewer's questions and prepare the famous people's answers, so that the programme runs smoothly. Encourage them to refer to the text for further ideas and to ensure that facts are correct. When the planning is complete each group should be given time to rehearse and practise their broadcast.

The drama

Below is an example of how a broadcast might be presented. For the purposes of illustration, I have used J. K. Rowling's Harry Potter books as the focus.

Children's roles   Presenter, interviewer, Harry Potter, roving reporter, Hermione, Ron, Aunt Petunia, Hagrid. (Roles can be doubled up, for instance Hagrid and Ron could be played by the same child.)

The presenter might begin by saying: 'Welcome to Delve Deeper, the programme that reveals more about your favourite characters. Tonight we pose the question: Harry Potter – myth or legend? With us in the studio are the two closest friends of the boy who has been called a genius, and later, we meet Mr Potter himself. Let's hand over to (child's name) to interview them now.'

The interviewer now introduces and asks questions of Hermione and Ron, such as what their first impressions of Harry were, when they first noticed something different about him, etc. The questions should relate to the storyline of the book and the answers should be given in character using only the information in the book – i.e. it is not permissible to embroider facts, or talk about a Quidditch match which J. K. Rowling did not write about!

The interviewer now passes back to the presenter who might say: 'Well, after those fascinating insights into Harry Potter's mind as seen by his friends, let's go over to 4, Privet Drive where I understand that our reporter [child's name] is with Mrs Petunia Dursley, who seems to have a very different view of the situation.'

The reporter interviews Aunt Petunia.

Back in the studio the interviewer might ask 'Well, Ron, what do you make of Mrs Dursley's claims that Harry Potter is a danger to her son?'

Next the reporter might interview Hagrid, perhaps providing further insight into the story characters by saying 'We were going to interview Mrs Dursley and Hagrid together, but it has proved impossible due to the violent reactions Hagrid expressed when this was suggested. He has agreed to be interviewed in this wood, and I must say I rather wish I had Mr Potter's powers at this moment – it's decidedly spooky.'

Finally Harry is interviewed in the studio. (See *Further ideas* for ways of involving the rest of the class.) The presenter rounds off the programme, which might finish with suitable music.

It is valuable to discuss the children's presentations after they have been seen by the rest of the class. Encourage constructive criticism and comments about actual features (rather than 'It was good.') Questions to focus on might be:

*   Were all the characters' responses true to the book?
*   Has the programme made you look at any of the characters in a new light?
*   If you had not read the Harry Potter books, would the programme make you want to do so?

Further ideas (Reception–Year 6)

Television panel/live audience   The rest of the class can become involved in the above TV presentation by becoming the live studio audience, applauding and asking questions, though this means that the characters on the guest panel have to be able to answer confidently, unless they are briefed as to the questions beforehand and have prepared their answers.

Key Stage 1 version   A simpler version of the above drama can be carried out with Key Stage 1 children using stories such as *The Three Little Pigs* or nursery rhymes. Interviews, even if extremely short and simple ('What were you doing when you saw the spider, Miss Muffet?') give children practice in presentation skills and in seeing events from another viewpoint. They also help the children to consolidate facts and sequences.

Dance

The Christmas story

An alternative to the nativity play, this dance for young children allows them to tell the story of Christmas through movement and mime.

Suitable for Whole class, Reception–Year 3.

You will need Choreographed music: 'Agnus Dei' from Fauré's *Requiem*. Suggested alternative music: any flowing sacred piece, such as a carol sung by choristers. Doll wrapped in white to represent the baby Jesus.

Introduction

Although the 'Agnus Dei' is not a Christmas piece, its beauty, reverence and pace matched the mood I wanted to convey in the dance. The dance is very much a mimed story, so is easily adapted to other music. As there are many recordings of Fauré's *Requiem* and the speed of different conductors will vary, the words are given below as a guideline to the movements. The timings relate to the recording I used, which is by The Cambridge Singers conducted by John Rutter (Collegium Records, 1988, COLC 109).

You will need to choose children to play the following roles: the Angel Gabriel, Mary, Joseph, three innkeepers, three shepherds, three sheep, three kings.

The pace is slow and children should be encouraged to slow down their movements to fill every bit of the music, rather than rushing and then waiting. Before the dance starts Mary should stand alone in the middle of the space.

The dance

0.00 *Orchestral introduction* Mary in place. Gabriel enters, flying gracefully and slowly. Circles Mary, who watches in awe. Gabriel points to heaven and to Mary to explain what is to happen (that she is to be the mother of the Christ child). Mary kneels down and nods to show she understands. Gabriel flies away.

0.18 *Agnus Dei, qui tollis peccata mundi* Mary runs to fetch Joseph, brings him to the centre of the space, mimes flying, points to heaven and herself to explain the angel's message.

0.33 *Dona eis, dona eis requiem* Joseph puts his arm around Mary. All other children (including those with roles) now mill into the area to represent the crowds at Bethlehem. The three innkeepers position themselves in three separate places where they will easily be seen by the audience and stand still, in contrast to the moving crowds (who should not block them). Joseph and Mary move through the crowds looking for a place to stay.

0.50 *Agnus Dei, agnus dei* On the first *Agnus*, Joseph and Mary stand in front of the first innkeeper and Joseph makes a large, clear mime of knocking three times on the door. Innkeeper opens door clearly and mimes shaking the head firmly and slowly to show there is no room.

1.01 *Qui tollis peccata mundi* On *tollis*, knock on second door and repeat mime with second innkeeper.

1.11 *Dona, dona eis requiem* On first *dona*, knock on third innkeeper's door. This time the innkeeper nods and Mary and Joseph go in. All children now walk to back of the dance area and sit down. At this point Mary needs to find the baby Jesus doll for later.

1.27 *Agnus Dei, qui tollis peccata mundi, dona, dona eis requiem* Shepherds enter, walking around the space at leisure, their sheep following on all fours, or feeding.

1.51 *Sempiternam requiem* Shepherds and sheep lie down to sleep and stay very still.

2.03 *Lux* On this beautiful pure note, all remaining children apart from Mary and Joseph rise to a standing position at the back and lift their arms slowly to become the angels. Hold until the note is finished.

2.09 *Lux aeternum, luceat eis, luceat eis Dominum* Angels fly gracefully and slowly around the shepherds and sheep, who watch in wonder.

2.29 *Cum sanctis tuis in aeternum, quia pius es* Angels fly gradually into a circle apart from three, who fly to the front ready to become the three kings. Shepherds and sheep follow into the circle, walking after the angels, who lead them to the back and sit down again.

2.51 *Cum sanctis tuis in aeternum, quia pius es* The three kings search for the star, hands shielding their eyes. One points to it. They form a small circle and bow regally to one another, then reverently mime picking up their gifts. They form a line one behind the other.

3.13 On the four loud organ chords the kings walk majestically to the back carrying their gifts proudly.

3.26 Silence – everyone very still, ready to form the final tableau.

3.35 *Requiem aeternam* Angels fly slowly from back and take their place in the tableau – this could be a line, a semi-circle or whatever looks right for the area you are using.

3.50 *Dona eis Domine* Shepherds and sheep move forward and take their places.

4.04 *Et lux perpetua* Kings take their places.

4.16 *Luceat, luceat* On the first *Luceat* kings and shepherds kneel; on the second angels slowly raise their wings.

4.32 *Luceat eis* Joseph, and Mary carrying the baby, enter and take their places in the centre of the tableau.

4.45 *Orchestral conclusion* All gradually depart, first angels, then shepherds and sheep, then kings, leaving Mary, Joseph and Jesus in the middle as the music ends.

Further ideas (Reception–Year 6)

Miming to music Dancing a story is a useful way of consolidating the sequence of events for young children. Challenge groups of four to cast themselves as Goldilocks and the Three Bears, the Three Little Pigs and the Wolf, or the Three Billy Goats Gruff and the Troll, and see if they can mime their way through the tales while some suitable music is playing in the background, such as Gounod's *Funeral March of a Marionette*. Prokofiev's *Peter and the Wolf* is an ideal example of a story matched with music, and young children can mime the different animal parts while it is played.

Shakespeare For older children, some of Shakespeare's plays provide wonderful material for movement, such as the magical scenes in *A Midsummer Night's Dream* and *The Tempest*. Shakespeare used many songs in his plays of which various recordings are available, and the plays themselves, of course, have inspired composers to write pieces specifically about them, such as Prokofiev's, Tschaikovsky's and Gounod's versions of *Romeo and Juliet*.

Art

Cinderella's banquet

Printing skills and other techniques are used to create the table setting for the sumptuous banquet provided at the ball where Prince Charming and Cinderella danced. This can provide a striking display when complete.

Suitable for Whole class in groups, Reception, Years 1 and 2, but older children could make a more sophisticated version and the subject matter is adaptable to any story that features a feast.

You will need Easiprint™ polystyrene sheets; pencils; printing inks; rollers; trays; paper tablecloth; white card; felt tipped pens; glue; squares of white cotton cloth (about 20 cm sq); plastic cutlery; gold spray paint; paper plates; food magazines; scissors; fabrics and assorted collage materials.

Introduction

If they do not already know it, tell the story of Cinderella to the children. When it is finished, talk in more detail about the ball. It must have been very special if Cinderella wanted to go to it so much. Couldn't she have gone in her old dress? Could anybody go? What kind of people would be there? What would they do there? What would the room be like?

Having established that this would be a high-class event for the rich and titled, explain that we are going to make the food and table settings for the beautiful feast that the guests would have when they needed a rest from dancing. Discuss what would be on the table and what there would be to eat. Divide the class into four equal groups.

The art activity

Group 1 Tablecloth Give each child a 10 cm square of Easiprint™. On it, ask them to design a simple shape which has something to do with the story of Cinderella or the ball (pumpkin, mouse, glass slipper, wineglass, etc.). They can draw this on scrap paper first before using a pencil to carve it into the Easiprint™. (If a child carves too deeply and breaks the Easiprint™, stick it on to a piece of stiff card.) Help the children to apply ink to their printing blocks with rollers in colours of their choice. Spread the paper tablecloth out and print the designs on to it in a pattern (my class chose to print them in a border around the edge in sequence, leaving the middle of the cloth plain to show up the food.) Leave until thoroughly dry.

Group 2 Plates and food Give each child a paper plate and encourage them to decorate the rim only, using felt-tipped pens. The best results come from bold repeated patterns, such as can be achieved by colouring in each fluted indentation in the plate's edge with two alternate colours – metallic gold and black look particularly striking. Children then cut out the food from magazine photographs or fabrics. Encourage balanced meals (in terms of colour as well as nutrition!) Some children might be able to make the foods look slightly 3-dimensional by sticking them over screwed-up tissue paper, using wool for spaghetti or screwed up balls of green tissue for peas, etc. Glue the foods to the plates.

Group 3 Napkins Each child needs a 20 cm square of white cotton cloth and a 5 cm Easiprint™ square. As with the tablecloth, they design a printing block suitable for a napkin – a suitable motif might be an item of food such as an apple. (Initials are not a good idea as they will print in reverse.) Help the children to ink the blocks and print the napkins, and leave to dry thoroughly.

Group 4 Napkin rings and place labels   Each child will need two pieces of white card, 5 × 20 cm for the napkin ring and 10 × 12 cm for the place label. The napkin ring can be decorated with a printed block the same size as for the napkins above. The name labels should be folded in two, and the front surface (measuring 10 × 6 cm) decorated in felt tips with a border and a suitable name for a distinguished guest. My class collected titles by asking teachers and parents for examples (Lord, Lady, Sir, Dame, Admiral, Professor, King, etc.) and then added their own name, making all surnames double-barrelled. Thus Fred Smith would become The Right Honourable Frederick Bassington-Smith, and so on. Great fun, though the names need to be copied carefully!

Teacher-Cutlery   For the final touch, the teacher or other adult can take the plastic cutlery outside, place it on newspaper and spray it with gold paint. Only the side that will show on display need be sprayed.

When all the components are finished they can be displayed on a table or vertically on a wall – use peel-off sticky pads cut into small pieces to secure the cutlery.

Further ideas (Reception–Year 6)

See if the three bears were right!   Strong links with science. Each child makes three thumb-pot porridge bowls: small, medium and large in size (though the largest should only be about 8 cm across to avoid breaking) perhaps to suit three teddy bears representing Daddy, Mummy and Baby bear. Fire and glaze the bowls, and then cook real porridge and eat it out of the bowls, seeing which stays hot for the longest time. When planning, take into account that the whole project will need to be spread over several weeks to leave time for the drying, firing and glaze firing to take place.

Bookmaking   A clear link with stories and with design and technology, suitable for Years 1–6. Children plan, design and make a small book for a specific purpose, perhaps relating to a story they have read – to contain spells, memories, poems, pictures, pressed flowers, or a story of their own.

Literacy

Thought tunnels and speech bubbles

A way to enable children to imagine and express another's thoughts verbally and in writing. 'Thought tunnels' is also a valuable winding down activity at the end of a drama lesson.

Suitable for   Whole class, able Year 2–Year 6.

You will need   Space for the class to stand in two lines; A2 and A4 white paper; crayons or paints; pencils; scissors.

Introduction

As a focus you need a story well-known to the children which you have been reading in class or working on in some other way.

To make a thought tunnel, the class stands to form two parallel lines of equal length, facing towards each other about a metre apart. They then decide which character from the story they would like to send down the thought tunnel. The character can be mentioned in the story (e.g. Pooh Bear) or imagined but not actually mentioned (e.g. Christopher Robin's mother).

The teacher chooses a child to represent the character. This is a good opportunity to allow a child who might usually be very much in the background to take on a key role without having to do anything difficult. The child walks slowly through the thought tunnel, and as he or she passes by them, each pupil can speak aloud the thoughts of the character. Those who wish to voice a thought may do so, but the thought tunnel offers no threat to those who do not want to participate.

The first time you try thought tunnels there may be silence, so you can ask the child to walk slowly back up the tunnel to give children a second chance to speak. If there is no response, talk about it with the children. ('What do you think he's thinking? I've got an idea. Shall I start?', etc.) In my experience, once children are used to the idea the thoughts are freely expressed.

Some points to help:

- it does not matter if two or more children speak at the same time;
- it does not matter if a child expresses the same thought as someone else;
- children may voice a view that they think the character holds but that may not necessarily be their own view;
- children should speak the actual words they imagine the character is thinking. For example, if Christopher Robin's mother is sent down the tunnel, as she passes a child could say 'I'm so glad I bought him that bear', but not 'I bet she's thinking she's glad she bought him that bear';
- thought tunnels are adaptable to any story, and thoughts expressed can be light-hearted or very profound. They offer a valuable strategy for older children to deal with difficult issues in stories.

The literacy activity

Thought tunnels help children to appreciate that there are many different views of one situation, and that sometimes it is not straightforward to decide what is right or wrong. It also helps them to realise that we do not always say what we actually think – for instance, we might lie because we don't want people to know what we really think, or we might say something untrue to avoid hurting another's feelings.

The exercise can now be consolidated in writing.

Divide the children into groups of three or four and give each group an A2 sheet of paper and crayons or paints. Each group is responsible for creating a portrait (full figure or face only) of a character from the story they are studying. Make sure that a good spread of characters with different views and personalities is represented.

When the characters are completed, display them on the wall and provide each child with a pencil, a pair of scissors and A4 sheets of paper. Invite them to draw and cut out some thought bubbles and some speech bubbles large enough to contain words which will be readable when they are displayed on the wall.

Children choose one of the characters and fill in both a thought bubble and a speech bubble for that character. They then stick the bubbles around the appropriate character portrait. They can make as many of each as they wish. When all the bubbles are in place the portraits can be used for class discussion.

Further ideas (Years 1–6)

Paintings

Display some reproductions of any paintings which include people. Invite the children to stick thought bubbles around them (using Blu-tack™) to express what they imagine the characters are thinking.

Interactive display   Display the portraits of characters made by the children, and/or the reproductions of paintings, in a central area of the school, and provide boxes containing thought bubbles and speech bubbles, Blu-tack™ and pencils for anyone to add to the pictures. Alternatively provide filled-in speech and thought bubbles and invite children to fix them to the correct character.

See Feelings – Literacy for related ideas.

Captain Hook

Captain Scott

Figure 22

Suggested Further Reading

Child Education, Infant Projects, Junior Education and *Junior Focus*, published by Scholastic Ltd, provide a wide range of practical ideas for teachers of Key Stage 1 and 2. Issues dating up to two years back can be ordered on 01926 816250 or 0845 850 4411.

Ways into Drama, Jane Bower, First and Best in Education Ltd, 1996.
Ten drama storylines and ten ideas for visual aids, with warm-up activities for Key Stage 1 and 2.
ISBN 1–860–832–41–5 Orderline 01536 399011

Creative History Activity Packs, Jane Bower, David Fulton Publishers Ltd, 2002.
Six practical packs of ten workcards addressing Key Stage 2 History through Art, Drama, Dance and Literacy. Many ideas adaptable for Key Stage 1.

> *Egyptians* ISBN 1–85346–940–8
> *Greeks* ISBN 1–85346–944–0
> *Romans* ISBN 1–85346–945–9
> *Tudors* ISBN 1–85346–861–4
> *Vikings* ISBN 1–85346–942–4
> *Victorians* ISBN 1–85346–875–4

Creative Science Activity Packs, G. Alan Revill, David Fulton Publishers Ltd, 2002.
Six practical packs of ten workcards addressing Key Stage 2 Science through Art, Drama, Dance and Literacy. Many ideas adaptable for Key Stage 1.

> *Light, Dark and Colour* ISBN 1–85346–947–5
> *Materials* ISBN 1–85346–946–7
> *Minibeasts* ISBN 1–85346–943–2
> *Predators* ISBN 1–85346–874–6
> *Rocks* ISBN 1–85346–862–2
> *Trees and Plants* ISBN 1–85346–941–6

Art in the Early Years, Kristen Ali Eglinton, RoutledgeFalmer, 2003 ISBN 0–415–29846–6.
Comprehensive book exploring Early Years art education and offering twenty practical art experiences for young children.

Teaching Art to Young Children 4–9 (Second edition), Rob Barnes, RoutledgeFalmer, 2002 ISBN 0–415–25474–4.
Balance of principles and practice offering specialist and non-specialists guidance and choices.

Teaching and Learning in the Early Years (Second edition), edited by David Whitebread, RoutledgeFalmer, 2003 ISBN 0–415–28048–6.
Chapters on each area of the Early Years curriculum, including a chapter on art by Jane Bower.